The Baptismal Mystery and the Catechumenate

RICHARD NORRIS
AIDAN KAVANAGH
L. WM. COUNTRYMAN
GAIL RAMSHAW
MICHAEL W. MERRIMAN
ROGER J. WHITE
WALTER L. GUETTSCHE
ROBERT BROOKS

The Baptismal Mystery and the Catechumenate

EDITED BY Michael W. Merriman

THE CHURCH HYMNAL CORPORATION, NEW YORK

Copyright © 1990, Michael W. Merriman.
All rights reserved.

The Church Hymnal Corporation
800 Second Avenue
New York, NY 10017

3   2   1

Contents

Introduction by Michael W. Merriman   6

I.   *The Result of the Loss of Baptismal Discipline*   20
RICHARD NORRIS

II.   *Catechesis: Formation in Stages*   36
AIDAN KAVANAGH

III.   *Formation in Salvation History:
How the Scriptures Form Christians*   52
L. WM. COUNTRYMAN

IV.   *Formation in Prayer and Worship
Living the Eucharistic Prayer*   72
GAIL RAMSHAW

V.   *Formation in Social Justice and Ministry*   79
MICHAEL W. MERRIMAN

VI.   *The Role of the Bishop in Christian Initiation*   96
ROGER J. WHITE

VII.   *The Catechumenate and
Christian Formation of the Parish Community*   110
WALTER L. GUETTSCHE

VIII.   *Post-Baptismal Catechesis*   140
ROBERT BROOKS

Bibliography   165

Introduction

MICHAEL W. MERRIMAN

The National Liturgical Conference, *The Baptismal Mystery and the Catechumenate,* took place in February 1988 at Grace Cathedral, San Francisco. Grace Cathedral and the Associated Parishes for Liturgy and Mission were the sponsors. The conference was inspired by the action of the 1985 General Convention directing the Standing Liturgical Commission to prepare a practical plan for the catechumenate and by Associated Parishes' growing conviction that renewal in the Church must begin with baptismal formation.

These papers were delivered at the conference and are now offered to the Church as a basis for using the rites of the catechumenate and related formation processes passed by General Convention 1988 and now available in the 1989 edition of *The Book of Occasional Services.*

The authors of the papers represent a variety of experiences with the catechumenate and more than one model for using it. It seems, therefore, important to preface the papers with a brief discussion of how the SLC and, therefore, General Convention understand the catechumenal process.

What the Catechumenate Is and What it is Not

The Catechumenate is more process than program. It is a means of structuring the experience of conversion into Christ and formation in Christian practice. Please note that it is the *experience* of conversion which is structured. Conversion is the work of God and cannot be structured or programmed. Even the process of baptismal formation, or catechumenate, cannot be given a form beyond a basic structure and some general principles of implementation, because it must be adapted to the needs of the individuals participating and the local parish community in which it takes place, and to the movement of the Holy Spirit.

The structure is a series of stages of varied and often indeterminate length, each concluded with a transitional rite. (General Convention, recognizing the value of such a structure, has approved parallel structures for the preparation of baptized people for Confirmation/Reception/Reaffirmation, and for the preparation of parents and godparents for the baptism of infants and young children.)[1] The stages and rites of the catechumenate proper are as follows:

Stage 1. The Pre-catechumenal Period... *Rite 1.* Admission of Catechumens

Stage 2. The Catechumenate .... *Rite 2.* Enrollment of Candidates for Baptism

Stage 3. Candidacy for Baptism ...... *Rite 3.* The Sacraments of Christian Initiation

Stage 4. Post-baptismal Catechesis

For a fuller description of the four stages see the section "Concerning the Catechumenate" in *The Book of Occasional Services,* Second Edition.

---

[1] It should be noted that in some parishes and dioceses baptized persons have been included in the catechumenate. The Standing Liturgical Commission believes that this is inappropriate because the texts of the rites are clearly for those who have not been baptized. They would devalue the baptism of such persons.

This process is expected to take a substantial amount of time in most cases. It cannot, however, be placed in a set time frame without giving the impression that conversion and Christian believing can be programmed. (There will be some persons whose background in Christian living and believing is such that it may be relatively short.) Most congregations I know of find it is about a year in duration for most people. The only events tied to the calendar are the Enrollment and Baptism. The General Convention has strongly urged that these be tied to I Lent and Easter, although I Advent and the Baptism of Christ are certainly good dates as well.[2]

Please note that this is no more than a structure. How the structure is filled out must be determined by other factors best arrived at in view of local needs. The content of the catechumenate is given, however, by the documents. It is scripture, Christian worship, prayer, and ministry for social justice.

The documents make clear that the study of scripture is as the record of the history of salvation. It is certainly the case that Bible content, origin of the scriptures, methods of interpretation, and systems for reading and meditating are to be taught, but salvation history is the over-arching subject. Learners are helped always to ask of a specific passage, "Where does this fit into salvation history?" Thus that history is to be learned first.

The history focuses on two events: the Exodus and the Paschal Mystery of the dying and rising of Christ. These two Passovers define the nature of the human relationship

---

[2]No other occasion of the Church Year provides so rich a context for Christian Initiation as the Great Vigil of Easter. For that reason we urge that adults and older children be initiated only at the Vigil, so far as that is possible.

with God. They define that crucial event called "conversion" both as it is initially discovered and experienced and as it is continually renewed in our life in Christ. So we are talking about a history which is a journey, a movement from one stage of life into the next.

But salvation history is not something found solely in the past. It is the on-going story of the People of God, and each individual needs to recognize its movements in his or her life and in the life of the community of faith. Thus we also focus on worship, prayer, and ministry for social justice. (Note that it is the Baptismal Covenant which gives us the four areas of concern.)

The methodology is reflection upon experience, in the light of the ongoing history of salvation. The individual's experience of worship, prayer, and ministry is the arena in which that story continues in our own time. That individual's story is also a part of the story of the larger community of faith.

Thus the catechumens will regularly participate in the worship of the community. They will be taught how to use the Prayer Book, and especially its forms of daily prayer and scripture reading in the Daily Office. They will be taught methods of prayer and helped to practice the various forms of prayer. They will be led into a process of discerning ministry, especially to the poor and neglected, and to see the opportunities for ministry in their daily lives.

(It is particularly important to note that they begin ministry during the catechumenate. Designs for the process which place such activities after Baptism are missing the chance to develop Christian ministry at an early enough stage that the catechumens will understand it as an essential part of Christian practice and have ample time to develop and reflect upon the ministries to which God is calling them.)

MICHAEL W. MERRIMAN

The curriculum for this process is the Bible, more specifically the Sunday lectionary. Week by week the lectionary gives us a portion of the scriptures. The catechumens and their sponsors and catechists reflect upon salvation history, prayer, worship, and ministry for social justice in the light of those scriptures.

Some people have expressed concern about the term "social justice" used in the catechumenal and parallel rites. Some of this comes from an assumption that "social justice" is being used as a synonym for "social action," and some from a concern that it would be read that way by people who are afraid of social action, especially in its 1960's manifestations.

The term refers specifically to the last three promises in the Baptismal Covenant, just as salvation history applies to the credal portion of the covenant and the first two promises following the Creed to worship and prayer. "Social justice" and our ministry come together in proclaiming Christ, in loving others, and in striving for justice and peace and respecting the dignity of every human being. Catechumens and others, indeed the whole Church, need to have before them Christ who was anointed to preach good news to the poor, and the fact of their own incorporation into Christ. In Baptism we are anointed by water and the Holy Spirit as Christ-bearers to preach and live that good news in our own time.

The reflection on experience model means that that which has not yet been experienced is not available for reflection. That is why most places using the catechumenate now dismiss the catechumens from the Sunday liturgy after the sermon. One cannot experience the Eucharistic action as a non-offerer and non-communicant. Catechumens do not witness baptisms and confirmations for the same reason. (It may be necessary on occasion for catechumens to be present but it will be found an undesirable, if needed, anomaly.) Note that in the parallel processes for people already baptized the candidates are communicants; they *do* reflect upon the sacraments and liturgical rites of the baptized, and are not, of course, dismissed.

This process cannot exist if it is considered merely one of the options going on in parish life. It has to be seen as central. If a parish has no baptismal candidates (or at least infants to be baptized and baptized adults moved to make their reaffirmation) that is a clear sign that there is something profoundly wrong with its life and ministry. Why isn't it evangelizing and identifying potential new members?

This process will bleed over into other parish activities. Christian education of children and youth will turn toward the ongoing reflection upon their experience of prayer, worship, and ministry in the light of salvation history. Prayer groups will take the Sunday scriptures as the starting place for their work. Vestries will begin their meetings by reflecting upon the parish's life in the light of the Sunday readings. Outreach ministry groups will see their work as an extension of the Baptismal Covenant. In fact, all the varied activities and groupings in the parish will take the nature of "Base Communities."

But we cannot define how these things will happen. We cannot put them into a "school year" sort of schedule. *And* the clergy cannot do this alone. In fact, the clergy can only serve as community gatherer, model for servant ministry, trainer of the trainers, and then step aside for the People of God to do their work.

The congregations that do the catechumenate, and parallel processes for baptized adults and youth and for parents of infants and small children, have found that, like the Holy Spirit, the catechumenal process cannot be packaged or controlled: not by the clergy, not by programmatic systems of education, not by the calendar, and not by the world.

• • •

The mandate of the 1985 General Convention to the Standing Liturgical Commission to develop, in consultation with the Education for Ministry and Mission department, guidelines "for a practical catechumenate" led to the presentation to the 1988 Convention of resolutions A098, A099, and A100, which were passed by the convention. The development of the guidelines for the catechumenate, and of additional parallel rites, was done by a committee appointed by the SLC which was chaired by SLC member Robert Brooks.

The committee's work in the triennium began with a survey of the catechumenal processes being used in various places and an evaluation of successes and problems which were surfacing. The most notable program is one going on in the Diocese of Milwaukee, where a number of parishes under direct guidelines from Bishop Roger White have been engaging in a form of the catechumenate for several years. There were also catechumenates in several parishes and at least one cathedral.

The primary questions being raised had to do with a clear definition of the catechumenate, what kind of process is needed for catechesis, and the place of already baptized persons in such a program. The resolutions passed by General Convention seek to give direction in those areas.

Resolution #A098: Principles of Implementation.

The definition of the catechumenate needed further clarification. Although the directions for its implementation in *The Book of Occasional Services* state that the catechumenate is for persons preparing for Baptism, the rites were also being used in many places for baptized persons preparing for Confirmation, Reception, or Reaffirmation. The direc-

Introduction

tions of this resolution specify that such rites are not appropriate for baptized persons. These additional principles make that clear. (It should be noted that they do not deal with the issue of preparation of older children, which we hope the SLC will deal with in the current triennium.)

When the SLC's committee first proposed this, the response from people in the Diocese of Milwaukee and other places was to acknowledge that such a rule is certainly right, but that they had found the structure of the catechumenate effective in preparing baptized persons for the laying on of hands as well. That response led to a further level of work which will be dealt with in the discussion of the resolutions which follow this.

The other question raised had to do with matters such as curricula and content for the catechumenate. The "Principles of Implementation" set out guidelines for those questions. The context of formation for the catechumenate and the parallel processes is in four areas: scripture, worship, prayer, and work for social justice.

Primary to this is the study of the history of salvation. This is envisioned as more than a study of the contents of the Bible. The scriptures are seen first as the story of God's saving action in history. Study of contents of the Bible and aids in reading and understanding are done in that context.

But salvation history is not simply something contained in the scriptures; it is an ongoing story in the lives of believers and of the community of faith. Therefore, the catechumens look at their own lives of worship, prayer, and ministry—both as individuals and as part of the community—as the place where the history of salvation is continuing. The principle curriculum in such a study is the community's shared reading of the scriptures: the Sunday lectionary.

The methodology of the catechumenate is reflection on experience. Thus the catechumens deal with that which they have and are experiencing. They reflect upon the scriptures that they and the congregation have heard read and preached. They reflect upon the worship in which they take part: Liturgies of the Word such as the *pro-anaphora* and the Daily Office. They reflect upon the prayer in which they engage, which means that they are being taught methods and types of prayer. They reflect upon the ministry they are doing and particularly that which occurs in their daily lives at work, at home, and in their communities. When they are introduced to organized social and ecclesiastical ministry, it is so they can engage in such activities and then reflect upon it. (In my own congregation this means that they are all engaged in outreach ministry and have been for some time before they are baptized.)

This methodology means that they do not engage in study of rites and sacraments in which they cannot take part. Thus their reflection upon Baptism, Chrismation and the laying on of hands by the bishop, and Holy Communion is not done until after they are baptized. This is the ancient content of post-baptismal catechesis or mystagogy.

The principles also make it clear that the catechumenate is not to be seen as a time-bound process which begins on a certain date and fills a specific portion of the year. New catechumens are admitted whenever they are ready. Their period in the catechumenate is determined by their need, not by the calendar. This means that in congregations which have a strong program of evangelization and a commitment to the catechumenate there will ultimately be catechumens most of the time. In such congregations the preparation of persons for Baptism will increasingly be seen by their members as a central and normal part of church life.

These principles suggest that the classic baptismal Gospel readings for Lent, found in the Year A Lectionary, be used every year when there are baptismal candidates for

Introduction

Easter. It gives guidelines for dismissing the catechumens each Sunday after the sermon so that they and their sponsors and catechists may engage in reflection upon the Sunday scriptures. (It has been found by many catechumens themselves that remaining with the baptized during the Eucharistic rite as non-participants is frustrating and unproductive.)

Resolution #A099: Preparation of Baptized Persons for Reaffirmation of the Baptismal Covenant.

As I mentioned above, the SLC's instruction that the catechumenate is appropriate only for unbaptized persons led to discussion with those who had found that the structure of the catechumenate was highly effective in preparing baptized persons for Confirmation/Reception/Reaffirmation. The Committee on Initiation looked at that structure and sought to find a way to use it while respecting the baptisms of those who are seeking to reaffirm their baptismal covenant.

This set of rites first states the structure: three periods of preparation each concluding with a transitional rite. This is, of course, a structure similar to that of the catechumenate. It looks like this:

Stage 1. Inquiry . . . . *Rite 1.* "The Welcoming of Baptized Christians into a Community."

Stage 2. Formation . . . . . . *Rite 2.* "The Calling of the Baptized to Continuing Conversion."

Stage 3. Preparation for Reaffirmation . . . *Rite 3.* "Maundy Thursday Rite for Baptized Persons in Preparation for the Paschal Holy Days."

The instructions make it clear that the content and methodology for this process is the same as that in the catechume-

MICHAEL W. MERRIMAN

nate, that is, reflection upon experience in the light of salvation history, worship, prayer, and ministry for social justice. It is clear, however, that these persons as participating members of the baptized community will be reflecting upon their lives as Christians in a number of areas which the catechumens will not encounter until after they are baptized. Therefore, in those congregations where it is desired to have the catechumens and the baptized join in some of their meetings, there will need to be times also when they meet separately. (I have found that this will work quite well in my own congregation.)

One exciting possibility in this process is that it opens to us the chance to bring all new members in a congregation together for a period of inquiry into the life of the local community. Several times a year, a period of inquiry can be announced for all those new to the parish. For several weeks they can look together at the worship, prayer, and ministry of the parish and its diocese. Opportunities for entering into parish life more fully can be introduced, as well as opportunities for Baptism and for Confirmation/Reception/Reaffirmation.

It will in many instances be the case that some in such an "Inquirers's Class" will not choose or need to choose some form of reaffirmation, and after being welcomed in the first rite they can go directly into those areas of parish life for which they are called and suited. (Some may find themselves being called as sponsors to those going on for Baptism or Reaffirmation, or called to be trained as catechists.)

You will note that this process is directed toward the Paschal Holy Days. It is hoped that the SLC will consider variations in these rites for reaffirmation at other times, but we still believe that the baptism of adults should be at Easter.

Also note that the third rite provides for an opening

address on Maundy Thursday which is far less clericalized than the one currently provided by the BOS.

Resolution #A100: The Preparation of Parents and Godparents for the Baptism of Infants and Young Children.

Here we have also a structure which parallels the catechumenate. It was suggested to its drafters by John Westerhoff's *Learning through Liturgy* (Seabury Press). Its stages are:

Stage 1. Pregnancy	*Rite 1.* "The Blessing of Parents at the Beginning of Pregnancy."
Stage 2. During Pregnancy and the time of Birth	*Rite 2.* "Thanksgiving for the Birth or Adoption of a Child."
Stage 3. From Birth to Baptism	*Rite 3.* "Holy Baptism"
Stage 4. Childhood catechesis in the family and the Church.	

There are several things to note about this process. Its first rite is from the BOS, with suitable modifications when both parents are involved, and the two other rites are from the BCP without change. The process expects the parish to be actively welcoming to those who have children and who are contemplating children. Parents will be encouraged to notify their pastor as soon as pregnancy is determined.

The model of reflection on experience in the light of salvation history, prayer, worship, and ministry for social justice is again given for this process, as is the Sunday lectionary as the basic curriculum. In this case, those being prepared (the parents and godparents) have been baptized

MICHAEL W. MERRIMAN

so their experience includes the sacraments. Their experience includes also pregnancy, birth, and parenting.

Those involved from the parish community will need to include trained catechists, godparents, any children in the family, and persons who are parents themselves.

This process will also need adaptation when the child is to be adopted and when the process does not begin during pregnancy.

It is also important to note that the process assumes that children will receive Holy Communion at their baptism and from then on. That this is a natural and essential part of the child's on-going life after Baptism is presumed by the guidelines.

• • •

All this material is to be found in the 1989 edition of *The Book of Occasional Services* just published by The Church Hymnal Corporation. The Education for Ministry and Mission unit at The Episcopal Church Center is in the process of producing materials for implementing these processes.

It should be apparent that a parish which takes this seriously will find a number of things happening: Baptism and its related reaffirmation rites will become the central activity of the congregation, the clergy will have to turn to lay persons as catechists and leaders for these processes, evangelism will be focussed on initiation and ministry rather than mere church membership, and parishes will develop an ever increasing number of persons actively involved in outreach ministry and steeped in the scriptures.

Acknowledgements

I wish to acknowledge those who made the conference, and thus, the publication of these papers possible.

Alan Jones, Dean of Grace Cathedral, and Mrs. Nancie Oyama provided the initial financial support from the cathedral's Oyama Fund. The members of the Council of Associated Parishes for Liturgy and Mission first conceived the idea of the conference and provided encouragement, support, and much of the leadership. Several other groups in the church gave their endorsement. They include: The Standing Liturgical Commission, The Church Divinity School of the Pacific, The Association of Diocesan Liturgy and Music Commissions, and the Lay Academy of the Diocese of California.

Mr. Frank Hemlin of the Church Hymnal Corporation encouraged the publication of the papers and assisted with his enthusiasm for the project.

I.

The Result of the Loss of Baptismal Discipline

RICHARD NORRIS

[1] Poets take out poetical licenses, we are told, which entitle them to fudge merely literal truth for the sake of deeper and more searching insights. I do not know where these licenses come from, or where a person goes to take them out; and in any case, since I am not a poet, I have no right to one. There is, however, a kind of licence I have always wanted—one which, I think, is proper to academics—a licence, namely, to take any question that is set before one, to declare it wrong-headed, and to rephrase it in accordance with one's own prejudices. And such a licence I propose to exercise today.

I have been asked to address the question of "the result of the breakdown of baptismal discipline and formation." Now this question, like all questions, makes some assumptions. One of them we can all agree about. A knowledgeable visitor who inspected the life of Christian churches in the United States today could hardly fail to notice an absence of anything like the discipline and formation that accompanied Baptism in the early centuries of the history of the Christian movement. Furthermore, such a visitor might well suspect that this void—for such indeed it is—is related, or (better perhaps) correlated, with other phenomena in the life of these societies, with certain unfortunate conditions that prevail within them, or with certain problems that they face. And this suspicion too we might reasonably share. Nevertheless it would be imprudent and simpleminded, on the basis of this inspection and the suspicion to which it gives rise, to suppose that the conditions and problems noted are simply the *result* of the absence of baptismal formation and discipline. Much more likely is the hypothesis that the problems on the one hand, and the "breakdown" on the other, are historical siblings which accompany each other, not as cause and effect, but as the offspring of common parents.

The question, then, is not one about the "result" of the "breakdown" of baptismal formation and discipline. The question is rather: <u>in what sorts of circumstances does the absence of such formation and discipline make sense?</u> With what state of the Church does it cohere, and what way of modeling or perceiving the Church does it fit? And the advantage of posing the question in this way should be clear. In the first place, it dispenses us from the self-indulgent habit of damning the past merely because we can see good reason for departing from its ways. There may after all have been circumstances in which the disappearance of the primitive baptismal formation and discipline made perfectly good sense.

But then—and more importantly—it forces us in the second place to see what it is that we are really saying if we call for a revival of baptismal discipline and formation. We are saying, in fact, that the circumstances of the Church's life today have changed to such a degree that the absence of baptismal formation and discipline no longer makes sense—that, indeed, the realities of Christian existence in the contemporary world are in significant ways more like those of the Ancient Church than they are like those of two or three or ten generations ago. The fundamental question is not one of liturgy or of catechesis (for after all, the liturgy of Baptism and the practice of catechesis have *not* disappeared in the Church—are we not all baptized, and did we not all go to confirmation class?); it is ultimately a question of what sort of church is presupposed by the practical *function* that Baptism and catechesis actually perform, and how the church is to live and to see itself in *this* world.

I ask your leave, therefore, to proceed not by chasing down the effects of a certain alleged cause, but by contrasting two rather different conditions and pictures of the church and correlating each of them with the practice of Christian initiation that characterized it. At that point it will become possible to inquire circumspectly what a revival of baptismal formation and discipline might signify for the churches now.

[2] First, then, let us turn our attention to the picture of the Church that emerges in a setting where what we are calling "baptismal formation and discipline" was practiced, if not with a vengeance, then at least with deliberate and serious purpose. To this end, I call your attention not to a liturgy (for I know little of liturgics and have never been able to keep all the baptismal anointings straight in my head), nor to an account of the elaborate catechumenate of, say, the fourth century, but to a couple of curious chapters in a work written around the turn of the third century. I refer to the *Paidagogos* of Clement of Alexandria, which is a sort of handbook for the newly baptized, devoted to

explaining how they are to live under the purifying tutelage of the divine Word. In the opening section of this work we have, not an account of the initiatory process, but a long and partly polemical interpretation of its meaning; and while Clement is, no doubt, eccentric in his way, his argument offers, if we not only follow it but analyze it, an honest picture of the functional meaning of the initiatory process and of the picture of the Church with which it cohered.

Clement's theme, of course, is *paideia,* which we can translate for our present purposes as "training," or perhaps even as "discipline." He notes at the very start that *paideia,* as the word itself suggests, is intended for children, and then identifies the children whom Christ trains as us: "We are the children."[1] By way of stressing this point, Clement searches the scriptures for places where the members of God's people are characterized as simple, innocent, and immature. He notes that Jesus called his followers children, and lambs, and even chicks. He insists, however, that these epithets should not be interpreted to imply that believers are persons of limited mental capacity. They point rather to two characteristics. One is simplicity and its concomitant, teachability; for the truth is, he writes, "that perfection is with the Lord, who is always teaching, and infancy and childishness with us, who are always learning."[2] The other characteristic is that of being, so to speak, new on the scene. Believers are described by such odd styles as "sons," "children," "colts," and the like, "to show the youth of humanity in Christ,"[3] to show that they are "free and new-born," and that they constitute a "new

---

[1] *Paid.* 1.5.12.
[2] *Ibid.,* 1.5.17.
[3] *Ibid.,* 1.5.15.

RICHARD NORRIS

people."⁴ Now one does not have to look far to find out whence this enthusiasm for the figures of childhood and infancy derives. Clement drops a clue when, with admirable restraint, he denies that the Lord's words, "Be converted and become as little children,"⁵ refer to "regeneration." He moves sidelong towards the point when he says that he has no objection to believers being called "simple ones" because they are children, since "the new minds, which have newly become wise, which have sprung into being according to the new covenant, are infantile in the old folly."⁶ The point finally emerges, however, in an explicit way as Clement avers that God has "begotten them again by his Spirit to the adoption of children."⁷ It is, then, Baptism in which the mother, the Church, gives birth to these children—that is, to newborn children of God, who share the status of the Son of God and gladly accept the training, the *paideia,* that their much elder sibling lavishes on them. Baptism is the fulfilment of the promise which the Spirit gives through the prophet David: "I have said that you are gods, and all sons of the highest."

These children, then, are called so because they have undergone a radical transition which can only be described in terms of rebirth. Indeed, Clement gets himself into trouble because the figure of childhood seems to consort ill with his own sense of what is involved in this abrupt, and profound, transition called Baptism. "Straightway," he says, "on our regeneration, we attained that perfection after which we aspired. For we were illuminated, which is

---

⁴*Ibid.,* 1.5.14f.

⁵Matt. 18:3, cited at *Paid.* 1.5.12.

⁶*Paid.* 1.5.20.

⁷*Ibid.,* 1.5.21.

The Result of the Loss of Baptismal Discipline

to know God."[8] God's work in Baptism is variously called *charisma*, illumination, washing; it cleanses sins, it remits penalties, it confers the "holy light of salvation,"[9] and above all it identifies us with the Christ whose images we are to become. So Clement must admit that Baptism and the faith that receives it are together the very substance of salvation: the baptized person "is delivered forthwith from darkness."[10] But then someone is bound to ask—and people did ask—how such a person is still a child, with growing and maturing to do? Clement's answer is, I suppose, the obvious one; at any rate it is roughly the same as Paul's. Baptism does indeed confer salvation wholly. It snatches the believer out of one form of life, one set of relationships, into another; but it does not, for all that, change the environment in which the believer's existence is embedded. It actualizes eternity, but only under the forms of time;[11] so from one point of view, salvation is present, while from another it is still to come, and the believer must continue to be nourished on the milk of the Word, while awaiting the day of that solid food, that meat, which is the "clear revelation in the future world." Thus the image of the child, the newborn, fits after all; for one would not say that a child is less than a human person, and yet there is training and growing to be got through before that truth is perfectly manifest. And in this way we get back to where we started: to the *paideia* which Christ, the Word of God, provides for those who have come through the waters and are living the new life.

---

[8]*Ibid.*, 1.6.25.
[9]*Ibid.*, 1.6.26.
[10]*Ibid.*, 1.6.27.
[11]*Ibid.*, 1.6.28.

RICHARD NORRIS

Now Clement does not bill this discussion as a consideration of what happens liturgically in the rites of initiation; and indeed one might read the whole passage and never quite realize that a definite ritual of initiation is presupposed by it. Nevertheless it is clear that what he has to say refers to a concrete and common experience, a "happening" of some sort, that he expects his readers to have shared—to have in common with him and with one another—and indeed this experience serves for him to *define* what they have in common as Christians. He is, then, addressing people who have gone through a transition, crossed a line, which can meaningfully be treated in the sorts of terms Clement employs, people to whom it makes sense to speak of rebirth and illumination and salvation because they have been through a process—a liturgy and a formation and a discipline—whose issue can plausibly be interpreted to them in precisely such terms. They are newborn children of God into whose lives enlightenment and salvation have come. And the question we have is this: how do such people see themselves, individually and as a body? How do they locate themselves in their world?

[3]   The first thing to be stressed, I think, is the nature of the line that Clement sees himself and his fellow Christians to have crossed. The way in which he speaks of Baptism makes it apparent that the transition which the initiatory process represents has more than one dimension and can be described in more than one idiom.

For one thing, of course, it is a transition which must be described, as Clement does describe it, in *theological* terms. It marks a fundamental alteration in a person's way of being related to God. That is what is conveyed in all of Clement's talk of "sonship" and "rebirth." When he says that believers are "children," he is using a metaphor that others had employed to describe the state of Adam and Eve in Paradise, and I suspect he knows it. The baptized, as he sees it, are fresh from the hands of God, remade, and recommencing the human story in accordance with the plot it had been meant to follow. Others may know of God and seek God; and indeed, if Clement is right, God has taken pains to be revealed to every people. But believers in Baptism become a part of God's household; they are adopted as God's children. Baptism marks a fundamental change in one's *way* of standing before God.

But then in the second place, this transition that Baptism marks can be described in psychological terms, in terms of its subjective meaning to the people who experience it. No one can read accounts of classical Christian initiatory procedures—whether in Hippolytus and Tertullian, or in sources that derive from an age that favored more elaborate arrangements—without being struck, not merely by the symbolic power of the things that were done, but by the personal and psychic costliness of the process. And this combination—of symbolic power and costliness—meant that initiation involved, to one degree or another, a kind of reconception of oneself, the sort of thing that we nowadays describe as "consciousness-raising." One did not pass through *this* transition without daring, and being willing, to see something new when one looked in a mirror. The plausibility of this new self might, because of circumstance or disappointment or failure of resolve, suffer; people might avoid Baptism and hang about forever as catechumens because they did not want to undergo the strains of *being* this new self. But in any case Baptism was a psychic reality, a turning point in the story of one's interior life.

And finally, in the third place, this transition that Baptism marks must be described in social terms. In fact it creates a community, or rather, a collection of related communities. In other words, the effect of Baptism in Clement's world is to generate that "we" which he keeps using with his readers. "*We* are the children," he says, and the "we" is not just anyone who chances to peruse his words. It is the baptized, whom this transition sets together and, of course, sets apart as a "new people". And it is important to see that it is the reiterated *event* of Baptism that defines and marks the boundaries of this community. We might tend to delimit the Church by reference to a set of beliefs; but we would be unlikely, in doing so, to recognize that the beliefs in question are simply the baptismal confession as it is regularly expounded in the catechesis, and that the importance of them is simply that they name and describe what it is that Baptism involves people with: God, Christ, Spirit, resurrection, forgiveness, hope. What defines the community is not an ideology, but an engagement with God in Christ who, naturally enough, is named in the event in which the engagement happens: Baptism. The Church is the community which lives out the life whose seed and beginning is Baptism; it is a social explication of the meaning of Baptism, a meaning that is enacted and so reiterated weekly, for slightly different purposes, in the sacred meal.

Looking at these three dimensions of the "sense" of Baptism as that emerges from the pages of Clement's little book, we can see two recurrent themes. The first is that Christian initiation, with the formation and discipline it involves, marks, for Clement, a definite boundary: a boundary in people's relation to God, a boundary in their inner sense of who they are, and a social boundary that marks out a "new people"—a people who live out the human enterprise in a new way. The second theme can be summed up in the two words "child" and *paideia*. Clement will not allow that Baptism needs supplementation of any sort; it sets people in the way of salvation firmly and surely. The

The Result of the Loss of Baptismal Discipline

baptized *are* "children of God". Nevertheless they are *children,* and the living out of the new life is therefore, in his eyes, an affair of continuous learning and growing. To put the matter briskly, what Baptism creates is a collection of disciples, apprentices of the divine Word, whose common life is, in every sense of the term, a *practice.*

Now on this picture we need to reflect—carefully and, for that matter, critically. The baptismal community as Clement pictures it is not, when one peers closely at it, a phenomenon that we find very familiar. In spite of the fact that he was, in his time and place, a notorious liberal, and quite possibly suspect in some circles for just that reason, he is clear in his mind that the Church is not a religious institution in the service of its society; it is *another* society, living a new and different sort of life, which one enters only through a personal revolution—i.e., a turnabout, a conversion—and which for that reason is inevitably set apart in its world. So much the operation of baptismal discipline and formation entails and assures. The Church is "different," and deliberately and necessarily so. But more than that, Clement does not envisage the life of this odd community, as we normally do, in terms of "ministry," but in terms of discipleship. It is a collection of people whose business it is constantly to rehearse a divinely authored play whose first actual, full performance will occur in the Age to Come. What its members are presently engaged in is the enterprise of learning their parts; baptismal discipline and formation constitute an event to be sure, but they also constitute a continuing *process* of *paideia.* Christ "is to us a spotless image; to him we are to try with all our might to assimilate our souls."[12]

I do not mean to suggest that Clement simply ignored

---

[12]*Paid.* 1.2.4.

questions of what we call "ministry." He did not. He recognized an official ministry in the Church, composed of elders and deacons, and no doubt acknowledged the persons who held these offices as the leaders and rulers of the community. Interestingly enough, however, he defines these two ministries in relation to the central business of *paideia* and discipleship, and he therefore regards them as public and focal "symbols" of the ministry that all relatively mature Christians exercise: that of "assisting" Christ by "improving" human affairs.[13] <u>Ministry, then, whether official or unofficial, is a subordinate concern. It exists to foster discipleship.</u> Indeed ministry is simply an extension of the service which the Church offers converts in the processes of baptismal discipline and formation.

[4] Here then is a picture of the Church and its life that not only consists with, but derives from, a serious practice of baptismal discipline and formation. That is, it is a picture of a Church whose sense of itself is formed by the institutionalization, at the very center of its life, of an initiatory practice, the character of which, as experienced, becomes a metaphor for the Church itself.

We know, however, that after the fourth and fifth centuries this practice, for various reasons of different orders, gradually faded. Some of these reasons may have been trivial, and some, whether trivial or not, are doubtless irrelevant to our concerns. Nevertheless a new situation arose in which the baptismal liturgy was, as the phrase goes, marginalized, and the Church at the same time assumed a different aspect, and one consistent with that fact. How shall we characterize that "different aspect"?

To begin with, I am inclined to think that the most

---

[13]*Stromateis* 7.1.3.

The Result of the Loss of Baptismal Discipline

important circumstance or condition with which this marginalization of Baptism cohered is quite simply demographic. Baptism's loss of centrality is correlative with the gradual appearance of societies in which, for practical purposes, everyone was, or was regarded as, Christian. One might, of course, look for other factors as well. The methods by which, on the whole, the barbarian nations of the west were "converted" in the Dark Ages did not, to say the very least, give a prominent place to baptismal discipline and formation; and the North African theory of original guilt, popularized and elevated to dogma by Augustine of Hippo, seemed to require, as a matter of mere prudence, that the normal subject of Baptism be an infant—on whom, of course, baptismal discipline and formation would have been wasted. For all that, it seems to me that the practice of baptizing infants exclusively could have arisen only in circumstances where everyone was expected, as a matter of course, to be a Christian; it is demography, not theology, that coheres with "the breakdown of baptismal discipline and formation."

The logic of this new situation can be stated in a phrase: Baptism ceased to differentiate. In reviewing Clement of Alexandria's little baptismal discourse, I noted that for him Baptism marked a *transition,* and that this transition had more than one dimension. It could be—and was—described at once in theological, psychological, and social terms. When, however, the religious demography of East and West alike underwent its fundamental shift, two of Clement's ways of talking simply ceased, automatically, to make sense. If Baptism made a social difference, that was only in the case of children whose parents had neglected to accord them the supreme advantage; and if it made a psychic difference, it was only as recollected—at the time of Confirmation, say—and even then, the difference made consisted largely in a sense of having "grown up" in a normal way. Where once the initiatory rites had signified a break—the acquisition of a new world and a new consciousness—they now signified normal steps in the processes of socialization: making it from womb to world, or from childhood to puberty. Theologians might continue, in their tracts and treatises, to mutter obscurely of rebirth and such-like matters, but it was difficult for ordinary people to see what they were talking about.

Now it would be easy, in this company, to wax satirical about this change in practice and perception, but one has an obligation to resist that temptation. If there were time enough, I would like to call your attention at some length to the fact that we have—from the nineteenth century, to be sure, when religious demographics were just beginning to change again—a rough equivalent of Clement's little discourse on Baptism. F.D. Maurice, in his own way, reflects on the sense of Baptism. His way, however, is the converse of Clement's. Where Clement models the Church for us through a reflection on the experience of initiation, Maurice distills the meaning of Baptism out of reflections on the character of a Church that is everyone's natural home. His discourse is not less engaging, nor indeed less profound and perceptive, than Clement's. It evokes, indeed, a vision that, in another time, Clement himself might have delighted in. The ultimate difference between them lies precisely in their different experiences of what it means—putting the matter as crudely as possible—to "join" the Church.

But this difference does spell a disagreement in one's very perception of "Church," and it is that disagreement on which we must dwell here. The fact is that the demographic circumstances which marginalize the processes of baptismal discipline and formation also make it difficult to figure out

The Result of the Loss of Baptismal Discipline

how to use the word "Church" itself. Ordinarily, one employs a particular noun to differentiate the thing it refers to from something else; when one says "apple," one does not mean "orange." But in a world where everyone is a Christian, it becomes exceedingly difficult to employ the word "Church" in this ordinary way, if by it one simply means "the people of God", for in fact there is no longer any difference to be observed between the people of God and the society at large. The Middle Ages experienced this lexicographical problem in an acute way, when it could not decide whether it was headed by Pope or Emperor because the same collection of people was both Church and civil society. The solution in theory was to say that "Church" meant society in its spiritual dimension, while "State" meant the same society in its earthly and material dimensions. The practical solution, however, was simply to change the denotation of "Church." No longer did that word pick out the people of God from other peoples (except perhaps in the cells of learned monks and the studies of theologians); it was more usefully employed, in popular speech, to distinguish clergy, and no doubt monastics, from ordinary believers. Thus the word "Church" itself came habitually to be used in a way that did not include ordinary Christians in the scope of its reference. My copy of the *Concise Oxford Dictionary* can thus offer, among others, the following definition of "church": "organization, clergy & other officers, of a religious society or corporation; clerical profession." I recall quite vividly a time when ordination was described for me as "joining the Church."

No doubt it is true that this habit of speech represents, as I have said, popular parlance, and not doctrine. It is popular parlance, however, that informs people's actual perceptions, their ingrained responses and reactions to the word "Church." And the results of this particular lexicographical shift can be perceived on every hand. <u>If one cannot differentiate "Church" from the general society, then one will differentiate *within* the Church itself; and if Baptism will not, in such circumstances, differentiate, then something else will.</u> Of course the logic of this situation can play itself out in a variety of ways. The borderline may be that between the once-born and the twice-born, a distinction that, perhaps unsoundly, uses the very language of Baptism to separate one set of the baptised from another. Or the borderline may be set by Ordination, and people who, as their years advance, get serious about the faith may think it natural and inevitable to express this fact by seeking clerical office—"ministry," as we say in English. And this same logic informs the very protest which we raise against its implications. Our way of reasserting the primacy of Baptism is to talk about the "ministry" of the laity—where Clement, perhaps, would have preferred to dwell on the discipleship of the elders.

[5]　　　　　　But this brings us to our present situation—that of the Church in a so-called "post-Christian" culture, in which, all of a sudden, we find ourselves on the one hand talking about a revival of the classical disciplines and liturgies of Christian initiation, and on the other hand secretly rehearsing the doubts and qualms and resistances that any such course of action would create in our minds. Why is this?

The answer, I think, lies in the fact that neither of the situations I have described quite fits the circumstances of the Church as we know it. We do not live in a world where the general population and the membership of the Church are thought, at least in principle, to coincide; that by now should be fairly obvious, in spite of all the polls that tell us how numerous are the citizens of this republic who believe in God. Nevertheless, the Church is not, as in Clement's day, something new and a bit alien in its world. Indeed it continues to be "established" in the sense that people regard its presence as normal and even, for the most part, useful. It is neither the people *simpliciter,* then, nor yet "another people." It is perceived as, and it functions as, a given social institution that meets certain needs and provides certain services. The people associated with it are often, in a way, more like customers—consumers—than they are like members. Thus the Church is indeed "different" in the sense of being optional and not for everyone; but on the other hand it is very much built into its society and its culture as offering and performing an accepted, standard set of services—"the ministry of the Church to the world" we call it, which is a nice, ringing phrase for social serviceability, the new "mission" of the Church.

Now what, *in such a setting,* would the reintroduction of "baptismal formation and discipline" mean? For this is, I take it, the cash value, the true sense, of our question about the "breakdown" of such formation and discipline. To explain what the breakdown has entailed is in fact to specify *what one hopes to accomplish by reversing or correcting it.* And that turns out to be something rather like the restoration of the sort of Church Clement knew: a Church composed of disciples rather than customers, because its members have undergone a process of re-socialization, and a Church which is less an accepted social institution in a service-oriented economy than a quasi-society in its own right, the breeder of a genuine subculture that is capable of questioning the values and assumptions of the world around it.

RICHARD NORRIS

Catechesis: Formation in Stages

AIDAN KAVANAGH, OSB

I am asked to address you concerning the catechumenate as a structure, or catechesis itself (the content of the catechumenate), as *formation in stages,* and to reflect upon this experience.

I am happy to do this. But you should be aware of a few things as I do so.

For one thing, you should discount that I have any first-person singular "experience" of catechetical formation. I am not a catechist. I am something much less. I am only a religious educator. My experience in this endeavor extends back over a quarter of a century. My experience as a catechist has yet to begin. My suspicion is that there are really very few real catechists here. If you find one, take him or her to dinner, and listen closely.

The moral of this little *divertissement* is this: do not mistake a religious educator like me for a true catechist. A true catechist is a rare bird. He or she would never make tenure at Yale, for doing catechesis is not an acceptable academic endeavor, and often not a very acceptable ecclesiastical endeavor either. <u>Doing catechesis is rather an evangelical and liturgical endeavor, neither of which is academically rewardable.</u> You may teach Bible; you may even sometimes teach liturgics. But you really ought not link the two, on pain of being consigned to the anonymity of a denominational seminary deep in the wastes of wherever. But let it pass.

Another thing you should be aware of is a certain nervousness on my part in discussing catechesis (which presumes catechumens, who are people fairly well into their conversion to God in Christ) without any treatment of evangelism. Catechumens do not fall from heaven in Glad Bags. Leave out evangelization, which is the steady proclamation of the Gospel by life and word on the part of every member of the Church universal and local, and one of two things will happen. Either there will be no catechumens to catechize, or those whom we designate as catechumens will in fact be no such thing (in which case trying to do real catechesis in their regard will sooner or later lapse into just some more religious education). The danger is that when a real catechumen does show up, that is, one whose life has been upended by the grace of conversion consequent upon his or her having been evangelized from some unexpected quarter, we will not know what to do or how to do it. Sensing this, such a person goes, or is sent off, to seminary.

I suspect that about half of our divinity students at Yale are, if truth be known, functional catechumens rather than people of settled faith consciously preparing for ministry in communities of similar faith. They come to us in the academy seeking meaning for their lives, with one option being that this might *just possibly* assume ecclesial form through some type of initiatory acceptance of them. This is what

Baptism and Eucharist do for ready catechumens. But what we, in collusion with you, give them instead is Ordination. When this happens (and it happens all the time) confusion about personal faith, sacraments, ministry and Church begins to breed like fruit flies. Ordination gets confused with Baptism; laity get clericalized; theology gets mixed up with faith, catechesis with religious education; Indians become chiefs; seminaries become catechumenates; the priesthood of all believers becomes the presbyterate; and we wind up evangelizing no one but ourselves. I spare you more.

In case I forget to remind you again, the thesis underlying all my subsequent remarks is that this ever-deepening fatal circle is the result of initiatory disarray in our churches, and that initiatory reform and renewal is the only way to break out of the same circle. Nothing I am about to say will make much sense unless we together see that such an initiatory reform and renewal necessarily embraces three large parts: 1) evangelization, 2) catechesis, and 3) the sacraments of initiation themselves, beginning with Baptism and concluding with Eucharist. We cannot have any one of these three large parts without the other two. Without *evangelization,* catechesis has nothing to work with, and the rites of initiation in that case can only be dissimulated. Without *catechesis,* the initial conversion occasioned by evangelization (which is often deeply subjective, incommunicable, and euphoric) cannot be nurtured, steadied, broadened into a coherent world view and brought to ecclesial term. And without the *sacraments of initiation,* catechesis loses its primary focus, which, in D.H. Lawrence's words, is to put "a man in his wholeness wholly attending" at that awesome Table where the Source and Redeemer of all things sits with us as among friends at dinner. When all three lapse, the great Vigil of Easter becomes a three-ring circus for those with ecclesiastical tastes.

Catechesis: Formation in Stages

My task, however, is not to speak of all these three things, but only of one: catechesis as formation in stages.

With the foregoing, then, as context, the first thing we must remember is that catechesis is fundamentally *conversion therapy*. It is not education in ecclesiastical data. There is no doubt that education in a certain amount of ecclesiastical data needs to be done, but this must not be confused with catechesis. What catechesis does, by way of what I have called conversion therapy, is threefold.

First, *catechesis helps the convert reassemble his or her personality and life around the new center of gravity which is God revealed in Christ Jesus.* Beginning to believe in this new center of gravity has already upended the convert's personality and life quite before the convert has ever got to the catechumenate, as a rule. This being the case, the new convert's main problem is often a sense of disorientation and alienation from familiar values and persons—"oceanic" feelings which need clarification and direction in order to avoid the onset of depression, in which one's conversion may well sour into obsession with one or another part of the faith while missing the whole. The catechist must help the convert overcome initial confusion consequent on the grace of faith having struck deeply into the convert's previously established personality and manner of life. And the catechist must remember that appeal cannot be made solely to the convert's mind, but to the heart, senses, and will as well, for grace embraces all these faculties. This is, by the way, why early involvement of the convert/catechumen in appropriate *liturgical* engagement is so important a component of catechesis, for the liturgy done beautifully and with flair also embraces the same human faculties. Conversion therapy is a worshipful endeavor, and worship embraces the whole person. The convert, it must also be remembered, *is not ill.* He or she is simply exhibiting normal symptoms of passage through a life crisis, in this case, coming to faith in the Christ of God from outside and for the first time.

Second, *catechesis attempts to seduce the convert's initial, subjective, and largely incommunicable experience of faith into the public domain.* The catechist realizes that Christian faith is never one's own personal possession. Although it is indeed a gift of God to the individual, it is far more often than not a mediated gift, and it is always a gift that must be held by the individual in communion, in solidarity, with others past, present, and future. The grace of faith is the ultimate form of the gift of life, and life is a gift mediated to one by others and held in solidarity, in communion, with others past, present, and to come. Realizing this, the catechist coaxes faith out from its womb in the convert's own soul into that ecological system of faith and life we call the Church, the Body of God's Christ where the Spirit flourishes. Here, once again, one may see how the rich discipline of the Church's worship is meant to be the main context for deepening, supporting, and nurturing so public a faith; the most intense focus of that worship we call, after all, a Holy Communion. The catechist constantly seduces the convert's faith to deploy and consummate itself in this rite, into this life. The convert's faith, without ever ceasing to be his or her own, must grow into ecclesial form anchored at the Holy Table. This is why Christian tradition recognizes the Eucharist, not Confirmation or Ordination, as the "seal" of Christian initiation, for it is in the Eucharist that the nuptials of God with our fallen yet redeemed race are consummated unto the age of ages.

Third, *catechesis instructs the convert in basic discipline for living a Christian life.* This may be the hardest thing the

Catechesis: Formation in Stages

catechist has to teach, and the hardest thing a convert has to learn. In an age of "do your own thing," "fulfill yourself," "the one with the most toys wins," and relativized ethics, it is hard to tell and exemplify for anyone else that there are certain things a Christian simply does and does not do. One absolutely does *not* pray against others in the presence of the only One who sees into hearts. One loves especially one's enemies and always reveres the poor. One refuses to be eaten alive by work, money, and sex. One spends less time amid abstractions like world justice, more time in living justly day by day without counting on receiving justice in return. One loves God above all things, and one's neighbor as oneself. One knows and respects the Way of Life, and one also knows and respects the Way of Death. One washes the devils out of one's hair and, by God alone, keeps them out. One's "yes" means yes, one's "no" means no. One stands reverently in the alarming presence of the Living God. And one understands that even so great a sin as oppression drains the oppressor no less than the oppressed, making both victims. This is the way sin metastasizes in our lives. The catechist is a strong person who incites the convert to even greater strength for the Gospel's sake and for the life of the world.

    I hasten to add that these three things are what catechesis as conversion therapy does. They usually go on, *mutatis mutandis,* simultaneously as coalescing dimensions of the same endeavor. They are not sequential stages, but happen together at each stage on an ever deepening level. Allow me now to speak about *stages* in the initiatory endeavor.

Perhaps the clearest schema of the stage-by-stage nature of initiation is found in the 1972 Roman document known as the *Rite of Christian Initiation of Adults,* which goes into full effect in this country on the first Sunday of Lent. It speaks of four "periods of investigation and maturation" (7).[1]

The first period is called "precatechumenate," and it extends from the time of evangelization to formal entry into the catechumenate, when "the rite of initiation begins" (9). The "precatechumenate" is said to be "of great importance and ordinarily should not be omitted" (9). The content of this first period is not called catechesis, but evangelization: "in faith and constancy the living God is proclaimed, as is Jesus Christ, who [was] sent for the salvation of all. Thus those who are not yet Christians, their hearts opened by the Holy Spirit, may believe and be freely converted to the Lord. They sincerely adhere to him who is the way, the truth, and the life, and who fulfills all their spiritual expectations, indeed goes far beyond them" (9). "The whole period of the precatechumenate is set aside for this evangelization, so that the true desire of following Christ and seeking baptism may mature" (10).

What seems to be envisaged here is a series of sessions done either one-on-one between inquirer and evangelist, or in small groups. No syllabus is offered. A Gospel might be read straight through, or lectionary readings might be followed. The period is a less than formal one, it seems, meant to deal with both serious and perhaps occasional inquirers. But its content, whatever form the period takes, is not catechetical, not academic, but *evangelical.* The main purpose is not to do biblical exegesis; it is to let the power of God's Word itself begin its work in the hearts and minds

---

[1] Numbers within parentheses refer to the appropriate rubric, as contained in the *Rite of Christian Initiation of Adults.*

Catechesis: Formation in Stages

of hearers. The agency is not with the evangelist but with the Gospel of the Lord. This is a context in which reverence seems more appropriate than being smart. We are reminded of the power of the Gospel on its own merits, and of the deep and rich effect *reverence itself* can have on human perceptions. Beginning the whole endeavor with reverence before the Word written and incarnate is not a bad way to start a journey to the Holy Table. It may be a way we will find hard to learn. We seem to be fuller of talk than of reverence, which may be one reason we have so few catechumens, and why evangelism has by default become something of a dirty word for what religious reactionaries are up to. The precatechumenate may thus have as much effect on the Church's recovery of its own self-perception as on preliminary inquirers—another thing that would not be a bad thing.

The second period is the catechumenate itself, where things start becoming more formal. It begins with a public rite of becoming a catechumen, which is said to be "of very great importance" (14), and is done in the Church's solemn presence. Here catechumens and the Church enter into a covenant of sorts: "Assembling publicly for the first time, the candidates make their intention known to the Church; the Church, carrying out its apostolic mission, admits those who intend to become members" (10). Entry into a preliminary degree of communion which will eventually be consummated at the Holy Table begins here. "Catechumen" is thus not the name of a certain kind of infidel, but of a certain type of Christian who now assumes certain rights in the Church. Among these are the right to be nourished by God's Word, to take part in certain liturgical celebrations (excluding the Eucharist from the Prayers of the Faithful onward), to blessings and sacramentals, to marry as a Christian, and to Christian burial. With formal entry into the catechumenate, therefore, there is an *ontological* shift consequent upon the grace of faith: the new catechumens take on real rights in the Church as the Church acts to fulfill its "apostolic mission" in their regard. This is an ecclesiological matter of some theological moment and great pastoral significance. Quite before Baptism, the Church's catechumens have *already* begun to be reconciled to God in Christ—to partake of that reunification and divinization which is the common possession of all those who enjoy (not by their own merits) communion by faith and sacrament with God in Christ by the Holy Spirit.

The catechumen is therefore not merely an infidel on whom religious educators enjoy open season. The catechumen is an incipient member of that society beloved of God because bought by the blood of God's only Son. Before such beings, Christian instinct has tended to light lamps, burn incense, and kiss the floor, for they are cherished as icons of the inscrutable love and mercy of God. Like Adam and Eve; like the patriarchs and matriarchs; like Noah and Jonah, Moses and Aaron and Miriam; like Jonah and the prophets, Daniel in a hostile land, Mordecai and Esther in an alien court, Joseph oppressed by his beer-drinking brothers, Naaman the soldier with leprosy and faith, Susanna leered at in her bath by dirty old men, and Israelites fleeing into the desert and stomping Canaanites into the ground.

You will notice, perhaps, that all these images (and more) form the tradition of Lenten readings, and that they culminate in the rather massive readings at the baptismal Vigil of Easter, East and West. In the Roman system, for example, the first eight Vigil readings are all baptismal: a first creation, Abraham's obedience, the Exodus, God's love for Israel, a new covenant, life in God, clean water and a new heart, and Romans 6 about death and resurrection.

Catechesis: Formation in Stages

In the ancient churches it is clear that their veneration of those who are coming to baptismal faith is not at all less than those churches' veneration of the Sacrament of the Altar. In catechumens, the Church sees that very same reality which the Holy Table's food extrapolates sacramentally—namely, Christ's Body mounting the cross amid the world's jeers and ridicule; Christ's Body rising, disconcertingly, to new life beyond the grave. This is why the ancient churches yearly consummate themselves at the edge of the font and at the Holy Table—not in Lady Chapels, nor in the streets of Managua, nor in the museums of London, Florence and Rome, nor in sing-in Messiahs at Christmas.

The point is that <u>traditional Lenten reading systems provide us with important information about the general content and mode of teaching which should fill the several years of one's catechumenate.</u> The content is fundamentally biblical, and the mode by which it is communicated is according to the liturgical year in catechetical sessions which begin in celebrations of the Word—in other words, worshipfully (cf. 19.1). By this basic content and mode of presentation, the catechumens' imaginations are enriched and given a vast succession of images which concretize in the most practical and accessible ways the role of faith in forming their new lives. And it is from this solid biblical foundation that they approach ". . . a suitable knowledge of dogmas and precepts and also . . . an intimate understanding of the mystery of salvation in which they desire to share" (19.1).

In other words, it is from a perspective of God's Word worshipfully received that they come to doctrine, not the other way round; for beginning with doctrine and then moving to the Bible is precisely what reduces God's Word to an arid and incoherent pile of proof-texts, the *reductio ad absurdam* of which is Fundamentalism. It is also from a perspective of God's Word worshipfully received and internalized that catechumens come to view the world around them in all its created splendor and its fallen horror, not the other way round; for beginning with sin, death, and oppression and then moving to the Bible is precisely what rewrites that Word, reduces it, and subjects it to our own passions and ideologies of the moment, the *reductio ad absurdam* of which is a sort of secularized Fundamentalism that tells one *a priori* what biblical passages can and cannot be read, what words can and cannot be uttered, what concepts can and cannot be held. If they do nothing else, catechumens help the Church keep its life centered in God's Word, which heals and convinces of sin.

The third period is called the time of election. This is also called a time of purification and enlightenment, and it ordinarily coincides with Lent. The "elect" are senior catechumens who are chosen in public on the first Sunday of Lent to be initiated at the Easter Vigil. From this point onward the local church and its elect catechumens move, as it were, hand in hand toward the renewal of both at Easter. The time of Lenten election is thus less like an instructional period than it is like a six-week retreat in which catechumens and Church together remember and internalize the baptismal images that are laid before them; each image tells us all, once again, who we are and of what we are capable without the grace of faith. The covenant into which Church and convert entered when the catechumenate began is reaching its consummation in prayer and fasting and good works. Now the Church is not so much ministering to its catechumens; its catechumens are increasingly ministering to the Church as living sacraments of its own continuing need for conversion to God in Christ. The Church rediscovers its own reborn self in its converts, a rebirth without which its self cannot long remain faithful in him who rose from the dead, trampling Death by his death.

The fourth period is that of mystagogy or post-baptismal catechesis. I spare you comments on this since Robert Brooks is to devote an entire address on this period at the end of the conference.

The foregoing has been nothing more than the briefest sketch of the main catechumenal stages or periods. Allow me a few reflections in conclusion.

First, the catechumenate is a very old Church structure whose restoration is very new. In Roman Catholic churches, our fifteen-year old documents dealing with it are remarkably concise and clear, yet among its enthusiasts there is a lot of confusion, sentimentality, equivocation, and loose talk. It is often called a program, a process, a vision. Many regard it as yet another new movement (like Cursillo or Marriage Encounter) to renew parish life. I spend a lot of time cautioning against all this hoopla because it is inconstant, inconsistent, frothy, and (like so many offspring of pure good will) misdirected. Few have realistically prognosticated its effects on conventional church life, should it succeed. Were they to do so, I suspect many would have nothing to do with it, for it will surely change everything, to the confusion of the conventionally pious—clergy and laity alike.

Clergy will have to learn their Bibles inside and out. We will have to find lots of catechists, as distinct from religious educators and clergy, and turn over to them much of the fundamental operation of the local outfit. We will have to discover and learn to serve adult converts, or we will have no one to catechize and nothing to initiate them into; we will all just be standing around barren fonts at the Easter Vigil, holding hands and renewing our own baptismal vows like crazy in an orgy of liturgical autoeroticism. We will have to work a lot harder at a leaner and meaner liturgy in which biblical preaching is much more closely coordinated with the rites themselves; a liturgy less filled with banners and state trumpets, but more with font and Holy Table and Gospel book. We will have to shift the popular perception that Christianity consummates itself at Christmas around a crib, to a credible perception that Christianity consummates itself at Easter before an empty tomb, standing in water and covered with chrism.

We will have to evangelize, evangelize, evangelize. Then we will have to catechize, catechize, catechize. Baptism then will take care of itself. But all this presumes that we first believe what we proclaim, and that our catechesis is steeped in this faith—a faith which is paschal and baptismal to its core. Here may very well be the greatest problem of all: namely, the restored procedure of Christian initiation, from evangelization through mystagogy, may be more faithful than we are. The rites in all their stages will not do themselves, nor are we the Faithful presumed to be their objects; we are their agents. Without our faith-filled agency, the rites are no more than words on paper. I am chagrined to say it, but I suspect that the faith the rites demand may be more than we are up to. To implement them, the first thing that must happen is that we are going to have to re-discover that faith is one thing, theology and socio-political ideology another; the first saves, the latter do not. The Nicene Creed embraces Father, Son, and Holy Spirit in the Church which sanctifies because it is first sanctified; it does not embrace other gods, including Shirley MacLaine or political parties and ideologies.

The restored rites of Christian initiation also presume a

leaner and meaner Christianity. Wherever such a Christianity exists, as in Poland, Russia, and the Third World, it is growing by leaps and bounds, and it has converts in great numbers. Even in France, *where priestly ordinations have declined by ninety percent since the end of the Second World War,* vocations to strict contemplative monastic communities (a form of lean and mean Christianity) are up by seventy percent. The moral is clear: when the Church of Christ is faithful to the Word of God worshipfully received, it is invincible. When it is not faithful, it becomes indistinguishable from any other social unit: Rotary International with hymns, a whacky New Wave frolicking with Gnostics in Malibu or gurus in trees, or the reincarnated who have been everyone in previous lives except Rutherford B. Hayes.

Evangelization, catechesis in all its stages, and Baptism track very big game indeed, namely, the way the world is as it emerges from the coils of evil which wrap the human heart. This by itself is enough to intimidate many prospective evangelists and catechists, who come quickly to realize that this world has teeth and its roses thorns. It is not at all user-friendly. This may be one reason why we prefer to evangelize only other Christians, to catechize only children, to throw our hats in the air over worldly ideas and programs only after this predatory world has sucked them dry and slithered on.

A second reflection is this. If you felt nervous at my use of the word convert, or at my emphasis on Jesus the Christ of God and his relationship to the Holy One whom he himself addressed as "Father," I suggest in all deference that you consider going into mutual funds or graduate school rather than into evangelization or catechesis. For Christian initiation is about conversion to God in Christ; all we know about this God is revealed to us by that same

Christ; and Christian tradition is absolutely unanimous in holding that we only know the rabbi from Galilee to be the Messiah or Christ of God to the extent that the Holy Spirit reveals him to be so. Christ is not Jesus's family name. And this Jesus was not just a concept, or a movement, or a dialectical argument. He was and remains a male of the species, born of a female of the same species, who gave his life for us all and sits with us still at a Table where we consummate our baptismal death and resurrection in him. Son of the eternal Father no less than Son of our race by the best of our race, Mary espoused of Joseph, Jesus the Christ stands solidly among us, reconciling all things to his eternal Father; divinizing them; bringing them all home to their Source.

This is the taproot and foundation of that faith which upends lives and unravels personalities which succumb to it. Its effects are why we catechize. Its burgeoning presence is why we baptize and give thanks at the Holy Table. Its having become a corporate way of life is the way we live as Church—a People in its wholeness wholly attending, for the life of the World.

Restoring the catechumenate is a fateful step because, once restored, it will require the recovery of evangelism preceding it, and the refurbishing of our catechetical and initiatory polity centering on Lent and Easter. Many shifts and new foci, together with a recovery of what C.S. Lewis called "mere Christianity," will be necessary if all this is to happen. But as we labor at all this, we must remember that what we shall be working for is not the introduction of a tertiary new piety or a new but temporary movement or program. We shall be restoring nothing less than the Church itself to its fundamental business in the world—preaching the Gospel, teaching all nations, and dying and rising in Christ. It is a work worthy of God's grace in all

Catechesis: Formation in Stages

through Christ Jesus and the Holy Spirit, a work to which all are summoned and enabled by that same grace.

Permit me to conclude with an ecumenical parting shot.

As I grow older, I find two tendencies becoming stronger in me. The first is that I am growing more staunchly a traditional orthodox-catholic Christian largely as a result of the astonishing follies we embrace when this tradition is jettisoned or ignored. The second tendency is my becoming ever more convinced that the reunion of our churches will never come about as the result of committee reports on this and that; nor from commending what is called, tautologically, "intercommunion" to the unready, thus reducing the Eucharist to ecumenical High Tea; nor from treating Ordination politically as an issue of power rather than one of iconic service to the community of ecclesial faith in God Father, Son, and Holy Spirit. If we wait for ecumenical *rapprochement* to issue from these endeavors, I think that we may as well busy ourselves with contingency plans for what to do *after* the eschaton has arrived.

I do not wish to be contentious, but constructive and realistic. Realistically, what we need is rediscovery in all our lives of the Gospel of God in Christ as the sustained tradition, created by both saints and sinners under grace, as it has been delivered with astonishing dynamism and diversity for two thousand years and beyond. Tradition is not about past events. It is about present events which, *because they are present,* necessarily have a past. And such events enable a reasonable future.

Constructively, I suggest that vigorously restoring our churches' initiatory polity, from evangelization to catechesis to Baptism and first Eucharist in the appropriate paschal "ecology," is the best way to rediscover the Gospel of God in Christ in all our lives. Then we might have something to evangelize about, our catechesis might have fundamental content once again, and our initiatory sacraments might regain their power for the life of the world.

To do this together is to seek union at its source—in God revealed in Christ and affirmed by the same Holy Spirit which holds those of such faith together. The way to *ecumene* starts here, and here alone—in faithfully evangelizing *not* each other but the unevangelized; in catechizing *not* each other but those whom our common witness has begun to summon home. Then the one Baptism about which we all talk has begun to exist, and on that basis communion in one bread and one cup on one Holy Table becomes not an experiment but an inevitability. Then the trumpet we sound ceases to be uncertain in the world.

III.

Formation in Salvation History: How the Scriptures Form Christians

L. WM. COUNTRYMAN

There are two questions I hope to address this morning: the first is, "What general contribution can the scriptures make to Christian formation?"; the second is, "What form does that contribution need to take in the particular situation in which we find ourselves today in the Episcopal Church?" To answer the first question, I think we must look largely to the past, to see how our forebears in the faith have made use of scripture in this respect. That is not to suggest that they exhausted all its possibilities, but only that we can learn from what they discovered. To answer the second question, we will find it helpful again to look to the past, but this time less for examples to follow than for some light on how our own situation is unique and calls for new and different solutions.

To begin, then, with my first question: "What general contribution can the scriptures make to Christian formation?" It is instructive to look at the little glimpses we get in the New Testament of the process of formation among the earliest Christians. As you probably know, the complex and developed form of catechumenate which served as the model for the rites we are exploring here is not of first-century origin; it is a result of the needs and the creativity of second-, third-, and fourth-century Churches. The Church of the New Testament era, by comparison, appears to have been rather offhand in the way it prepared people for initiation. Luke, in the Acts of the Apostles, pictures new believers, Jews and Gentiles alike, as being baptized the very day they were converted.[1]

We do know, however, from Paul's letters, that there were traveling apostles who preached the Gospel, local teachers who gave instruction (Gal. 6:6), and other people, not further specified, who baptized converts.[2] The act of Baptism was surely not the end of the instruction process, especially when it was administered at the very time of conversion. Paul frequently reminds the addressees of his letters about things he had already told them while he was with them and about the personal example he had set them. Probably it took more than an hour or two to communicate all that he had to say; yet, we must also remember that many of his churches were founded during visits lasting no more than a few weeks. Apparently, one could communicate the essentials of the new faith in a very short time.

What did these early Christian missionaries try to communicate? Briefly, I think we may say that there were three areas of instruction: a sacred narrative, an ethic, and a theol-

---

[1] E.g., the Jewish converts on the day of Pentecost, Acts 2:41, and the Gentile jailer with his household at Philippi, Acts 16:33–34.

[2] Not necessarily identical with the apostle, for Paul declared that he had baptized few of the Corinthians and drew a distinction between the ministry of preaching and that of baptizing, 1 Cor. 1:14–17.

ogy or spirituality (there was no clear distinction between these last two in antiquity). The ethic they communicated, at least in what proved to be the Christian mainstream, was Jewish in origin, but universalized so that Gentiles did not have to cease being Gentiles in order to fulfill it. Christians excluded or relativized the Levitical purity ethic, which constituted, along with circumcision, the main barrier between Gentiles and Jews. Traces of this new Christian ethic are probably found in the vice catalogues of the New Testament Epistles and in the ancient Two Ways document, which survives in slightly differing forms in the *Didache* and the *Epistle of Barnabas*.[3] This emphasis on ethics was no doubt a result of the early Christians' awareness of their community life. As a strange new commingling of Israelites and Gentiles, they could no longer rely on shared cultural presuppositions to guide them in their common life. They had to become explicit and clear about ethics and to remind one another that, in Baptism, they had put off the old humanity and put on a new one which demanded a certain standard of behavior.

The theological dimension of instruction became necessary to help the new converts understand the full implications of what they were going through. Thus, the author of Hebrews, when he referred to the elementary foundations of Christianity, included among them "teaching about washings *(baptismoi)*" because the Christian washing *(baptisma)* had to be distinguished from other sorts of religious ablutions that the new convert might well have experienced or known about. He also included teaching about "laying on of hands and resurrection from the dead and eternal

---

[3]Cf. Philip Carrington, *The Primitive Christian Catechism: A Study in the Epistles* (Cambridge, England: The University Press, 1940), pp. 13–21.

judgment," suggesting that these, too, were connected with Baptism, either as accompanying rites or as consequences (Heb. 6:1–2).[4]

We get a solemn and beautiful example of this kind of theological or spiritual instruction in the Epistle to Titus. It is worth quoting in full for the way in which it crystallizes the significance of Baptism for late first- or early second-century Christians:

> For we ourselves at one time were also senseless, disobedient, erring, slaving for passions and for varied pleasures, living in vice and envy, despicable people, hating one another. But when the goodness and generosity of our savior God appeared, not as a result of works of righteousness that we did but in accordance with his own mercy he saved us through a bath of re-creation and renewal of Holy Spirit—something he poured out on us lavishly through Jesus Christ our savior, so that having once been set right by his grace, we might become heirs by hope of eternal life (Titus 3:3–7).

This clear vision of each person's past and future, emerging from God's grace and centered on Baptism, was a large part of what made Christianity a vital force in its world.

Our New Testament evidence suggests, however, that prior to, and more fundamental than, either the ethical or the theological instruction was the third type of teaching—namely, instruction in the Christian narrative. We get glimpses into it in such passages as the speech of Peter on Pentecost. Luke represents Peter as beginning with the

---

[4]Paul would have agreed that Baptism had to do with resurrection and the judgment; cf. Rom. 6:3–11.

Formation in Salvation History

immediately observable phenomenon of speaking in tongues, which he treats as a revival of prophecy already predicted by Joel. He moves quickly, however, to narrating the story of Jesus' death, resurrection, and future reign (Acts 2:14–36). We see the same kind of interest in narrative in Paul's brief reminder to the Corinthians about the substance of his teaching on the passion and resurrection (1 Cor. 15:1–8). The passage is little more than a bare list of the events, with only a minimum of interpretation. Above all, we see this concern for narrative in the Gospels themselves as expanded and interpreted versions of the basic tradition.

For the very earliest Christians, of course, this narrative was not to be found in scripture, that is in written form. They knew it from oral tradition, eventually reducing it to written form so that it became scripture for us. Yet, their scriptures, what we now call the Old Testament together with some of the Apocrypha and Pseudepigrapha, were important to them in the telling of the story. It was the ancient writings that enabled them to understand and explain why the story about Jesus was important for human beings. From the earliest times that we can still recover, they were already saying that it all happened "according to the scriptures." They quoted specific texts that they saw as being fulfilled in what Jesus had done and suffered. They borrowed images, such as messiah or suffering servant or Passover lamb, which they felt captured some of what Jesus meant. They claimed that the age-old good news of God's vindication of the people had been realized anew in the cross and resurrection, and they looked for its complete fulfillment in Jesus' return with glory.

This instruction, scriptural and narrative in character, was the heart of earliest Christian formation. We do not know how much of it took place before and how much after

Baptism, but it was their attachment to this story that made people Christian.

Scripture is not, of course, simply identical with narrative; there are many other kinds of literature included within it as well. Yet, narrative is a uniquely important component of scripture. It forms the framework into which everything else is incorporated. Even seemingly timeless materials such as the Psalms, the Song of Songs, and the book of Proverbs are attached to it by the fiction of ascribing them to David or to Solomon. Even the laws which made up the basic covenant code of Israel are incorporated, in the Torah, into a sweeping narrative that moves from the beginning of creation to the settlement of Israel in Canaan.

This arrangement of our scriptures corresponds to some deep human needs. Narrative is perhaps the single most basic way in which human societies identify and mark the topography of their cultural worlds. We tell stories about what happened in the beginning, where our ancestors' came from, what we were doing before we came here, what we are doing here, what dangers confront us, what failures we have endured or what triumphs achieved, and what hopes beckon us onward. From these stories, we draw conclusions, often unspoken ones, about past, present, and future. We know what kind of world we are living in by knowing what kinds of things have happened in it and what kinds of things we expect to happen. As the stories change, the world we are living in changes, too.

Jesus' parables show a highly sophisticated awareness and use of the power of story to shape world and, equally, to break it and to reshape it. A certain man fell among thieves. . . . A bishop passed by on the other side. . . . A priest did the same. . . . But a Mormon traveler stopped, got him to the hospital and agreed to pay whatever it cost to care for him. . . . Who turned out to be neighbor to whom in this case? Jesus' Jewish audience will have rebelled at least as much against his original Samaritan as Episcopalians against my Mormon substitute. Their stories told them that Samaritans were half-Gentiles, perverters of the true faith of Israel, enemies of the temple at Jerusalem, the one place where God had made his name to dwell. Yet, here is a Samaritan (or a Mormon) behaving faithfully and generously when a couple of leaders of the chosen people had failed to. One can accept the old story or the new, but not both. We want to keep the old one; and yet, we know in our heart of hearts, as did Jesus' audience, that the new story is perfectly plausible and that our older, simpler world will not quite work any more. We do not have to become Samaritans or Mormons, but we cannot any longer divide our world into a simple them (the bad folk) and us (the good folk). Our simple and unquestioning confidence in nation or in denomination is undermined.

Stories that whole peoples, such as the Christian people, can live out of over generations must necessarily be very rich and complex stories. The scriptural story is that and more. Sometimes it seems more distinguished for richness than for clarity. In the long run, that is probably more of a strength than a weakness. We cannot exhaust it quickly. It contains within itself the possibility of new understanding and of response to the challenges of new epochs. Still, we can lift up from it a coherent message, a Gospel which summons people to enter a new world and become at home in it—not the world of late-twentieth-century America, though we are far from indifferent to it, but the world of the Reign of God. To enter this world, by becoming attached to the scriptural story, is to see the realities around us with new eyes and to understand ourselves in relation to both God and world in a new light.

L. WM. COUNTRYMAN

It must be said that this does not happen just by the telling and retelling of a narrative as complex as that of scripture. There are too many places to take hold of the narrative, too many different texts that might vie with each other for central place. A religion which took Samuel hewing Agag in pieces before the Lord in Gilgal (1 Sam. 15:33) as the center of scripture would be very different from one that chooses the crucifixion of Jesus or one that puts the apocalyptic visions of the end of the world in that place. The Church, historically, has not only told the story in its full richness and complexity. It has also found a need to summarize it briefly in such way as to provide a kind of key, directing the hearer or reader to the points of highest significance.

Paul's tradition about the passion and resurrection of Jesus (1 Cor. 15:3–8) offers such a guideline—a simple listing of events held to be fundamental: "Christ died for our sins according to the scriptures and was buried and was raised on the third day according to the scriptures and appeared to Cephas, then to the Twelve. . . ." Peter's Pentecost speech offers another summary, emphasizing the death of Christ by God's foreknowledge along with his resurrection, exaltation at God's right hand, and second coming (Acts 2:22–36).

Every effective effort to proclaim the good news must distill and focus the narrative on the points that we see as of primary significance to our hearers. For catechetical purposes, the Church quickly found it necessary to produce relatively simple guidelines for the instructors, in the form of the *regula fidei* or "rule of faith" used in the second and third centuries, and for the catechumens, in the form of the baptismal creeds which superseded it in the later third and fourth.[5] We still find what they produced very useful. Yet, we must acknowledge that the specifics of, say, the Apostles' Creed were shaped by the circumstances in which it came into existence. At a time when Gnosticism had questioned the relationship of things spiritual to this material, created order, our creeds (and the *regulae* that preceded them) emphasized that the ultimate and true God, not some subordinate being, created this world and that this Creator God was also the Father of Jesus. The opening statements of the Apostles' Creed are nicely calculated to drive home just these points. Apart from the Gnostic challenge, the Early Church might not have felt it quite so important to emphasize God as creator. We thus become aware from the example of our forebears in the faith that it is necessary not only to lift up the essential Gospel in the long narrative of scripture, but to do it in a way that responds to the characteristic falsehoods of the environment in which we live.

All these considerations make it clear, I hope, that formation in scripture is an essential aspect of formation in Christianity—but that this does not mean simply turning individuals or small groups loose on the text to make of it whatever they can. The Church at large must struggle with its understanding of the narrative and determine what impressions it wishes to emphasize in handing it on. While the ancient creeds offer us important guidance in this, they will not settle all difficulties for people of an era drastically different from the one in which they arose. We shall have to recognize what summary guidelines we are already offering, sometimes quite unconsciously, and decide whether they are in fact what we want to be saying. We cannot expect to go much further in communicating the Gospel

---

[5]Cf. Joseph Crehan, *Early Christian Baptism and the Creed: A Study in Ante-Nicene Theology*, Bellarmine Series 13 (London: Burns Oates & Washbourne, 1950) and L. W. Countryman, "Tertullian and the Regula Fidei," *The Second Century* 2 (1982) 208–227.

until we learn to say briefly and with conviction exactly what we think is central to it.

Having found these keys, we shall then have to resist the temptation to dispense with the story itself in all its rich and confusing ambiguity and substitute for it our little summaries. The summaries can never become a replacement for the narrative itself; if they do, they will kill it and then die themselves of malnourishment. Our declared faith will no longer be rich enough to correspond to real life or to sustain real communities. Our rules of faith, ancient and modern together, are no more than keys to take back to the lock, maps to help us find our way around the difficult terrain, touchstones to help us tell the pure gold from its alloys.

With the help of such guides, we can immerse ourselves and ask those coming to us for instruction to immerse themselves in the narrative at large. We can expect that such an immersion will gradually transform our understandings and bring them more into conformity with the Gospel proclamation. It will not be a quick process, however. We must think of catechesis not as a time when Christians become fully equipped but rather as a time for establishing habits of study and gaining an initial grounding in the scriptures. This will make it possible for Christians to continue lifelong in an intelligent, faithful, and prayerful assimilation of the scriptural narrative.

No goal could be more Anglican. Everything that I have said can apply to Christian formation in any orthodox denomination, but our Anglican tradition has been uniquely shaped by the program of reading scripture in course in the context of prayer. When Cranmer took over the Daily Offices from the Benedictine tradition and presented them, newly Englished, to the whole people of God in the first Book of Common Prayer, he reshaped them not only by reducing them in number and complexity, but by making the reading of scripture their centerpiece. By following, for the most part, the canonical order of books in his lectionary, he also insured that the narrative element would have its full weight, year after year, as the introduction to and framework for the rest of scripture. At the same time, <u>by placing the scriptures in the context of prayer, not in that of Bible-study classes like the independents or of preaching like the Puritans, he implied that understanding of them must go hand in hand with a widening and deepening relationship with God and could not be simply an intellectual endeavor.</u> The joining of scripture and prayer together in the Office gave Anglicans henceforward the opportunity to immerse ourselves, to steep ourselves, in scripture and so to be transformed until our world becomes truly the world of the Gospel narrative and its world becomes truly ours.

In connection with baptismal catechesis, this emphasis on the scriptural narrative has yet another advantage intimately related to our church's Reformation heritage. It underlines that Baptism is truly a gift, not something that we earn by being good students or faithful probationers in the catechumenate. It does so because the narrative always begins with God, not with us. Whether in the grace of creation or that of the calling of Israel or that of our redemption in Christ Jesus, it is God who calls us into being and into relationship with him. God acts and we human beings respond, with varying degrees of understanding, appreciation, and thanks.

Thus far, I have been dealing with my first question, the one regarding the general benefits which the scriptures offer to the process of Christian formation. I have suggested that these benefits consist especially in the creation, through narrative, of a cultural world which shapes our grasp of the realities around us. It is important, however, to consider also the second question about the particularity of our contemporary situation and the ways in which we can best effect scriptural formation here and now. I think that our situation is unique and essentially without precedent in earlier ages. For much of our history, whether in Israel before the time of Jesus or in Christendom over the centuries in which it flourished, religion and society were indistinguishable. There was little occasion for the Church to think of itself as an independent institution or to emphasize its obligation for formation of its members. To grow up in ancient Israel or medieval Europe was to be formed religiously, culturally, socially, and politically all at once. This is not to say that the results were always good. It could be argued that there is an inherent contradiction in the notion of Christianity as a culture religion. Still, this was the situation over many, many centuries. For a person to experience individual conversion and a conscious formation in faith within this context, it was virtually necessary to become either a monastic or a heretic.[6]

If we look back beyond the Peace of the Church, however, I am not sure we shall find anything much more in tune with our own times. To be sure, the church of the first three centuries was, like that of late twentieth-century America, a voluntary association without formal connection to the state, existing in a society that did not understand itself primarily in Christian terms. There, however, the resemblance ends, for the ancient church was an *illegal* subsociety. While persecution, before A.D. 250, was sporadic and unpredictable and there were times of relative quiet

---

[6] I owe this observation, though in a more carefully nuanced form, to my colleague Professor Guy F. Lytle.

Formation in Salvation History

and openness, the Church never had the challenge of having to create its own boundaries. They were defined for it by the society at large. They were relatively sharp and clear. Membership was secret to some degree. The nature of the community itself was a mystery to many outsiders, despite the efforts of apologists to reassure the public that it was really quite harmless. Information about the exact beliefs of Christians was probably not easy to come by. There were a number of competing sects, sometimes with radically divergent teachings. If someone did learn enough and was moved enough to wish to become part of such a community, a longish catechumenate was a necessity both for the Church and for the convert. It was necessary for the Church in order to test the sincerity of a person who might later turn informer; it was necessary for the convert in order to learn the specifics of a faith that could be approached in no other way. In the 1950's, I became an Episcopalian in principle from reading books before I ever set foot in an Episcopal church; I don't think mine was a unique experience. That sort of "detached" conversion will not have been an option for most people in antiquity.

In short, the Church of the second and third centuries had a fairly clearcut social task to perform with its catechumenate: to assimilate people with little knowledge of the Church—and little other access to such knowledge—into an illegal and therefore sharply defined community. It had to be appropriately sceptical of their motives and commitment and it had to immerse them over a period of time in the new world to which they were being assimilated. Because the ratio of adult converts to offspring of Christians apparently remained high, the catechumenate, by assimilating these individuals, also determined the character of the Church as a whole.

When the Church was legalized under Constantine and

later became the official religion of the Empire, the situation changed radically. The fourth-century Church retained and even elaborated the catechumenate, but we should not suppose therefore that nothing much had changed. Everything had changed. The catechumenate had previously been the means of crossing a boundary marked out primarily by Christianity's illegal status. Now this same catechumenate began to define the boundary itself. The *disciplina arcana*, with its pretence that, in an increasingly open situation, Christianity was still as secret as ever, marks this new stage of the catechumenate as an artificial substitute for social boundaries that Constantine had broken down. The catechumenate still had to be long and demanding, of course, but to the degree that it had ceased to have an immediate and obvious function as providing an entry into an illegal and therefore secret society, it was in danger instead of becoming a barrier to be surmounted or a work to be performed, proving the worth of the successful and earning them passage into the Church.

If our revived and adapted catechumenate should come to be seen as a way of earning salvation (or even status in the Church), it would not be contributing to the proclamation of the Gospel. I think, accordingly, that we must be very careful to ensure that we are not unintentionally creating artificial barriers to make our society appear more elite or to suggest that human commitment is somehow of more interest to us than the grace of God. Baptism must remain the free act of God's grace. The instruction we receive along with it is a matter of helping us live into all that it has already secured for us.

If, however, we consider carefully the social situation of the modern Episcopal Church, I think we can see a way forward. The essential point is the very one already pointed out for us by the rites laid before us at this time, namely that those who will be coming for instruction are of the most varied possible description.

There was a time, rather recently, when we formed a part of the great, unofficial Protestant religious establishment of the US Adult converts typically came to us from other parts of that establishment, were already educated, through their churches and through the larger culture, in a certain common understanding of Christianity, and needed now only to be fine-tuned, as it were, in the peculiarities of Anglicanism. The Protestant establishment, however, no longer exists in most regions. It has broken apart in disagreements between liberals and conservatives, in disputes over religion and the public schools, in the tension between those interested in private spirituality and those concerned about social reform. One result is that <u>people raised Christian in most Protestant denominations are very poorly informed as to the nature of their faith—not only our own younger people, but also those who come to us as adult converts from other denominations. These constitute one large class of candidates for the new, revised catechumenate.</u>

Add to these, whose Christian understanding is vague and uncertain, an increasing number of adult converts who have had little prior acquaintance with Christianity in any form. Add those, at the other extreme, who have already had a good grounding in the faith, albeit not in the Anglican tradition. Add those whose acquaintance with Christianity has included ample indoctrination, but in forms of the faith which most of us would regard as seriously flawed, such as Fundamentalism. Finally, add those raised as Episcopalians who have come to feel that their grasp of their tradition is inadequate, perhaps only because it is somewhat inarticulate. The overall mix is formidably complex.

Yet, there is no need today for anyone to become an

Episcopalian in order to learn about Christianity in the Anglican tradition. There are books available. We should not pretend that our revived catechumenate has much to do with that of the second century, when there was no other route to knowledge of the faith. We should not pretend that there are clear boundaries around us, set by the larger social order and to be crossed only in this one way, or that all of our "catechumens" somehow fit a single mold. Indeed, they will range from people almost totally ignorant of the Christian proclamation to people who have already spent many years maturing in the faith but feel their lack of articulateness. The great issue, then, is to seek ways of educating people in the good news of the Gospel of Christ that do not draw invidious distinctions as to one's origins or prior degree of preparation, ways that are as accessible to the newcomer as to the seasoned faithful and vice-versa.

The study of our foundation narrative in the scriptures is ideal for this purpose because it need not exclude anyone nor be beneath anyone. The scriptural narrative is accessible at whatever level we are able to approach it. It ought to form the heart of every catechumenal program—not, however, in the form of intellectual study in an isolated sense. The Anglican tradition sets the reading of the Bible in the context of prayer, and that is where it belongs for us still. This removes the occasion for invidious comparisons between those who know more and those who know less and it refocuses attention where it belongs—on the question of how the biblical narrative is shaping and reshaping our world.

As I suggested earlier, we shall first need a summary of the narrative to focus our reading of it. I believe that we have one already at the heart of our Sunday worship in the Great Thanksgiving, most comprehensively the recounting of the story of salvation in Eucharistic Prayer D (BCP, pp.

Formation in Salvation History

373–74). It would be appropriate to begin here to interpret the scriptures with those seeking to be better grounded in the faith, so that it becomes clear that every aspect of scripture, in order to have its full force, is to be related to these central events and, through them, to our lives here and now.

The other great desideratum is a method of reading individual passages that can relate them both to the central themes of the story, as underlined in the Eucharistic canon, and to our own lives in the context of prayer. The classic Anglican model for this has been the Daily Office, and I believe that it can become so again if we help people to perceive its basic character. The Daily Office acquaints us with scripture by immersion, by the repeated reading of it until it has a chance to become for us a language, a world, a basic way of perceiving reality. This does not happen simply by magic, however; it happens by reflective reading in the context of prayer—that is to say, in the presence of God consciously acknowledged. The Daily Office, whether read privately in abbreviated form or, when possible, corporately in its full form, should probably become a staple element in our revived catechumenate.

Yet, I think that the Daily Office will not, in our rather hectic age, "work" by itself. We also need a method to help people assimilate scripture and not merely read it. We are used to learning by more intensive methods, and the scripture readings of the Daily Office, with their breadth and leisurely pace, may fail to make a sharp impact. I think we would do well to encourage people in a system of quiet reflection on scripture, based on the office tradition and focusing it more clearly. I propose the regular use of the following five questions:

1. What sort of material have I just read? (e.g., narra-

tive? law? poetry? prophecy? visionary literature? practical advice?)

2. Where does this passage belong in the great story of salvation, as laid out, for example, in Eucharistic Prayer D?

3. How is the situation presented here similar to my situation and that of my community?

4. In what ways does this passage challenge my presuppositions or those of my community? (This is more difficult to get at. It may be helpful to begin by putting the question the other way round: What in this passage seems crazy or pointless by my standards?)

5. What word of God do I hear at this time in this passage for myself and my community?

We should introduce this method of reading (or some other, similar expansion of the traditional *lectio divina*) in a setting where people can practice it together and share their responses without fear of seeming ignorant. By beginning in a communal setting, we give extraverts the necessary community support to learn a somewhat introspective method, and we encourage in all of us the sense that the learning and understanding of scripture is the business of the Church as community and not simply of individuals. Properly inaugurated, this can become an easily-used tool for most people. It refers us constantly to the basic scriptural narrative and then draws us back into the Church's living proclamation of the Gospel in praise and thanksgiving.

The scriptures, particularly in their narrative portions, are vital to any project of Christian formation because they create for us and with us a world that is quintessentially Christian in its basic orientation and yet also exceedingly rich in its openness to the here and now. It is the world of the Reign of God, in which we are summoned to live already, not as an escape from the world of the late twentieth century, but as a source of strength for living in it and seeking its transformation. As Anglicans, we seek a knowledge of scripture which proceeds from God in prayer and returns to God in prayer, all the while transforming us and our world as it moves through our daily lives. We should not settle for less. It is impossible, of course, to do it all in one year or two. We cannot complete the task even in a lifetime, if it comes to that. But we can begin to be learners. And as long as we are beginning to live in the Reign of God and sense that we are living more deeply into it as we go, we can afford to continue always as learners, sharing that role with the newest of Christians and the most seasoned alike.

L. WM. COUNTRYMAN

IV.

Formation in Prayer and Worship: Living the Eucharistic Prayer

GAIL RAMSHAW

It is difficult to describe how liturgy forms the faithful. At least I cannot say how this phenomenon occurs. Professional liturgists devoutly desire that participation in the liturgy does in fact form the faithful into the community of God. But we who are eager for the formation of persons as Christians must beware that we do not merely gun our engines, on the theory that more and better liturgy, like more gasoline, will get this church moving, for we know that there are countless people who regularly participate in Christian liturgical celebrations and whose lives appear to be untouched by the experience.

We speak autobiographically, or we probe Christian history, or we interpret studies, but we do not know how and when the liturgy is experienced as the vehicle for God's Spirit. We speak to one another only our hopes that the liturgy which has brought grace into our lives will do the same for others, children and adults alike. Many of the techniques for formation which are popular among newly converted adults are inappropriate for my daughters, still young children who were baptized as tiny infants. Yet I can hope that their weekly participation in the Eucharist will form in them an attitude of praise, prayer, and service which will join them to other Christians in an increasingly secular culture.

Simply said, here is the liturgical logic: that the weekly ritual of assembling around Christ in prayer for the world will form in Christian people the mind of praise and the habit of service. Prayer is to shape us by hope for compassion. Unfortunately, much of the prayer written by white middle class American Christians has been so dwarfed by psychological rhetoric that intercession has more in common with personal therapy than with baptismal formation. The nineteenth-century faith in Jesus as personal Savior has met the twentieth-century human potential movement, and this results too often in prayers about how I can be more fulfilled this week. To find a prayer for Christian formation, let us look to the classic Western Eucharistic Prayer with its elements of praise, remembrance, and petition, and let us ask together how to live the prayer.

Aristotle said that a story needs a beginning, a middle, and an ending. But the literature of this century indicates a world in which such naive order has been destroyed. Stories begin in the middle, proceed with a logic all their own, and stop without concluding. In many novels, the calendar day is the only shape given the protagonist's tale. The death of the omniscient narrator suggests a world in which we can speak only a private vision of personal values. The incoherent violence of recent movies seems to cement in American consciousness, rather than purge away, the terrible pattern of Vietnam, where our highest ideals began questionably, proceeded dishonestly, and ended "not with a bang but a whimper." Adopted children in a mythic search for origins locate their birth parents, discovering only one or two slight middle-aged aliens. Like digital clocks, we live minute by minute, the sweep of life obscured by the orange flashing figures, numbers as isolated as we ourselves.

How would it be, were we formed by the beginning of the Eucharistic Prayer?

In the first place, we would have assembled on Sunday. Endless orderless time would be benevolently laid before us in units we could grasp, and we would give priority to the first day of the week by assembling with others who shared this calendar of grace. Like the disciples in John's Gospel, we would gather on the first day of the week with sure knowledge that at such a weekly meeting God would be present to bless us. This is no small thing, this communal affirmation of a human order to the universe, this peaceful acknowledgement that our time begins together in God, this shared value that from such an assembly flows life in abundance. Assembling on Sunday is like acting out Genesis 1, in which the universe, rather than mindlessly expanding into more vacuum, is benevolently ordered for the good of humankind by a God who teaches us praise. Thus merely to assemble with the baptized on Sunday is to recreate the modern universe, giving it a beginning in God and a middle in grace, with hope for an end of fulfillment and peace.

The Eucharistic Prayer, like Sunday, situates the community in a graceful world. We begin by praising God. We acknowledge God as an Abba God, the loving parent who arranges the nursery to the child's best advantage, who protects the infant from final evil, who nurses, instructs, and chides better than all the human parents and all the mythic gods and goddesses who fill our lives and storybooks. God

Formation in Prayer and Worship

creates the world, we say. We form our community around this assertion, that the world has its meaning in and from God, and that as we are in God we participate in its meaning. God saves the world, we say. We form our assembly around this belief, that contrary to appearances, evil has been overcome by and in God, and that as we are in God, we together are saved. Were the assembled community to enter into this opening paragraph of praise, our formation as Christians would have made a substantive beginning.

"Humankind cannot bear very much reality," wrote T. S. Eliot, and one way that we protect ourselves is to forget. The old saw is true: women do not quite remember the pains of childbirth. That I was in pain I remember; what the pain was like to have made me scream so wildly, I cannot recall. We forget the sufferings of the race, the assassinations in our country, the quarrels in the family, and we try to relax in an easy chair with earphones gently playing only New Age music. Yet another way that we protect ourselves is to overlook. There is a man lying on the train platform, crying out in pain, but I am in a hurry; I must not miss my appointment; it might even be a set-up. It is as if each person has a certain capacity for pain, and it is usually quite filled to the brim, whether the pains be personal, familial, social, or political, and there is no room for the suffering of others.

To pray the Eucharistic Prayer is to be the community which focuses on the suffering Servant. In the center of the prayer we remember Christ, the one who heeded the cry of the man on the platform, even to his own death. We call to our remembrance, making the memory alive and well, that God is among us as one who serves the suffering ones. God sees human suffering and remembers it. And God's response to the cries in the emergency ward and around the world was to bind up our wounds, pouring on oil and wine.

To pray this prayer together is to take on the mind of Christ, to don with the name "Christian" the life-style of the Servant. Let the Church be the donkey on which Jesus lays the wounded man; we are to carry those who are newly anointed and communed. To pray this prayer is to recall, against our self-protective amnesia, the death of Christ, and to hear, in spite of our headset, the cries of all in need. John's Gospel teaches us that the meaning of the Last Supper is seen in Jesus' washing his disciples' feet. So we come to the table ready to serve.

Our culture is exhausted by its frantic search for community. No wonder our children are enchanted by reruns of "Little House on the Prairie," with its evocation of a mythic time when small neighborhoods of folk lived with shared values in communities marked by friendliness and concern. The reformed drug addicts visiting our schools eagerly petition everyone to join their enthusiastic campaign for a drug-free society, and I see in their fervor the old delight in group identity: "We are reformed druggies, we call you to our mission." Such a sense of group identity, such shared goals, such communal responsibility and support—these are increasingly rare in a society which seems overwhelmed by trying to embrace too much too fast. Now we do not look any longer to the pages of the *National Geographic* for pictures of foreign patterns of life; we see them across the hall of our apartment building.

To pray the Eucharistic Prayer is to invoke God the Paraclete. In this prayer we pray for the Paraclete to come among us, to make us one, to bring all the needy into our heavenly city. We pray that the Paraclete will continuously voice our concerns before God's throne, that there might finally be some action towards mercy and renewal. Together we pray for communion, and even in the prayer begin to enjoy the communion which we seek. But the communion of God's imaginings is so far beyond our own, that always in the Eucharistic Prayer we are drawn to a deeper sense of what human communion is: not wearing similar clothes or seeking the same entertainment, but discovering a bond of love which God alone can create.

We are formed by our culture to live in chaos without praise, in the moment without sympathy, and in lonely search for communion. To pray the Eucharistic Prayer is to praise God for a world mercifully saved, to remember the suffering ones as a faithful servant would, and to petition together so heartily for communion in this world that our lives naturally follow our prayers. Thus we learn not to molder away our lives watching television world without end, with its sound blocking out the needy world, its emptiness a symbol of our own barren lives. We join with a community that sings hymns on Sunday morning, that remembers Christ and hears the needy, and that in praying for communion becomes a community of servants.

The Eucharistic Prayer forms us by bringing us to God. For God is the Abba, ordering the world in mercy; God is the Servant, identifying with all the needy; God is the Paraclete, forming us into community. The doctrine of the Trinity need not be an archaic and sexist way to draw silly pictures of God. For Christians, the doctrine of the Trinity hints at the mystery of God and calls us into a human existence made in the image of this mysterious and merciful God. The institutional Church is always buying some new method for catechesis and some new theory of education, and the prophets on the edge of the Church are always calling out their prescriptions for conversion and reform. Yet no sooner have we sold our decade's soul to a method or a cause, than we see our convictions as limitations. The doctrine of the Trinity, which classically provided the Church with its outline for eucharistic praying, offers to the

Church also a program for catechesis and its inspiration for amendment of life.

How would it be were our catechesis and conversion formed by the doctrine of the Trinity? Here are some suggestions for our parish education and service committees. The families of the newly baptized infants would recommit themselves to regular eucharistic praise and service. Our children would learn the Bible stories of God's benevolent love and would hear the lives of the saints, who are co-servants with us, part of the community for which we strive. Mystagogical catechesis would be revived among us, with adults growing more deeply each Paschal season into the mystery of life with God. Rather than mirror the aimless race of contemporary culture, parish life would be marked by the beauty of hospitality and peace. The "least of these" would be the most honored in our midst, as we remember with St. Lawrence that the treasures of the Church ought not be the new copes in our sacristy, but the homeless in our cities. We would see every need, every sorrow, every stranger, with the eyes of a servant. We would stand together to support one another in the pain of seeing. We would break through the solipsism that sets in after the evening news by choosing one or two people who need our care, one or two cooperative efforts, and by working for the communion for which we pray.

These are only several suggestions, merely starters, for the Church's formation by the liturgy. We are to be formed by the Church's prayer to become such prayers in the world, such instances of praise, service, and community, such personifications of joy, sympathy, and hope. We are so formed, not by successful parish programs or popular media techniques, but by the Spirit of God, who draws us by God into God. May God, Abba, Servant, and Paraclete, teach us so to pray.

Formation in Prayer and Worship

V.
_____

Formation in Social Justice and Ministry

MICHAEL W. MERRIMAN

When the Council of Associated Parishes began dreaming of this conference two years ago, we were responding to several years of struggling with issues of ministry and church in relationship to the liturgy. In 1976 we asked ourselves whether, with the new Prayer Book in place, there was still anything for AP to do. "Why does the Church need Associated Parishes anymore? Everyone knows about balloons and confetti at the Eucharist and about using real bread and about pulling the altar away from the wall. What shall we do now?"

As we struggled with our purpose, our attention was drawn to ministry and particularly to the diaconate. In that order of ministry our old concerns for liturgy *and* mission surfaced and we became excited about the diaconate, much as some people today are excited about the catechumenate. Yet many people in the Church responded that since every priest is also a deacon, why start pushing for a separate and equal ministry of deacons. At that point we began to realize that something was getting in the way of the diaconate and we suspected that it might be priests. As we talked about the presbyterate we realized that no one can make sense of it because what we really needed to figure out was what bishops are. The suspicion of some of us was that, until we did that, the priesthood would not make sense because presbyters seemed useful only when bishops are not around. This discussion went on for two or three years.

Finally we spent a week with Richard Norris taking us through all of these issues. During that week, first Robert Brooks and I, who were already using the catechumenate, and then others on the AP Council began to be certain that we needed to be talking about Baptism.

Before we could make sense of the ordained ministry or of any other aspect of the Church (including the liturgy) we had to go back and find out what Baptism is. Finally the conviction has grown that to recover Baptism as the watershed event in the life of the Church and the individual, we have to discover what formation is.

Baptism, it seems, is one of those events which when looked at directly disappears. It is too complex an event to be isolated. Only when put into its churchly context of formation, ministry, and the life of the community does it take shape. I suspect that the catechumenate is like that as well. When we define it too much and program it too much and start printing too many books about how to do it, we then begin to lose it.

My way of talking to you today about the catechumenate is to tell some stories about my own journey in learning about the catechumenate—by telling some stories about what happens when converting people are involved in the life of the Christian community and particularly how formation in social justice begins to take place.

Formation in Social Justice and Ministry

Some years ago, a priest I knew was on his way home from some hospital calls. He realized he was in the neighborhood of a family who had just arrived in his parish the preceding Sunday, so he decided (on the off chance that they would be at home) to stop in and get to know them. The door was opened by the five-year-old daughter who, it turned out, was the only family member at home. But the little girl, having already been formed in Episcopalianism, immediately said, "Please come in," and she showed him into the living room, found a comfortable seat for him, sat down facing him, and composing herself said, "I'm so glad you could come, Father. We don't do nothin', and we don't hurt nobody."

I've always remembered that story, and it has been for me a paradigm of how the Church is seen by the world and to a great extent by its own members. Seen as a trivial institution, not often able to affect the life of the world, and engaging itself most of the time in activities and using its resources in ways about which the world doesn't give a damn. An institution which, when it does speak to major issues, most often gets its agenda and program from the secular world.

When we look at the Pat Robertsons and Jerry Falwells and their followers, we see groups with which many of us may have differences, but they do care about the major issues of the world and they have a vision of social justice which doesn't come from the secular world. We may feel that their ideals of justice are misplaced or wrong, but we are seeing one group of Christians in this country who have found an identity; they have a story, they have a clear vocation, they have a picture of how people ought to live, they are committed to it, they are converting people to it, and they are forming them in that way of living. They have

MICHAEL W. MERRIMAN

their own schools and their own media (and their own version of Disneyland, until the downfall of the Bakkers).

Where are the mainline churches? Basically we don't know where we are or who we are. We're pulled apart into competing sects.

When I was a parish priest, I became increasingly concerned about what I was doing and what was happening in my parish. The major factor that led me into my involvement with the catechumenate was when I went to work for Associated Parishes. After seven years in a parish in Texas, I had some time to look back, think and reflect . . .

The parish I had served was a small parish in a suburb of Dallas, a blue-collar suburb. The composition of the parish was a little different from your standard Episcopal parish because most of the people were low to middle income and very few had college educations. They had come to the Episcopal Church out of the "let's join the church for the children's sake" movement, and in reaction to the small town fundamentalist backgrounds they had come from. They saw the Episcopal Church as an alternative, and my parish had numbers of such adults coming to us to become Episcopalians.

I ran non-stop confirmation classes for adults. They were extensive sessions running eighteen weeks. I didn't just teach them the seasons of the church year and how to pronounce Sexagesima, and introduce them to Dorothy Sayers mysteries. We did lots of work on the Bible, and I prided myself on my success at helping them move away from their fear of the Bible due to their Fundamentalist backgrounds. We had a terrific liturgical life. Best of all was our pioneering the Great Vigil of Easter in that diocese. By my last Easter there, the Vigil was a larger service than that on Easter Day, with the Bishop and lots of baptisms and confirmations.

Formation in Social Justice and Ministry

In that parish we did lots of good work; we converted people, in a sense. We converted them from being lapsed Baptists or Methodist or whatever, into being Episcopalians, and good Episcopalians. We tried to be involved in social justice in a community which was not only blue-collar, but red-neck. But I began to realize more and more that people's attitudes toward their life and their relationships—how they used their time and their money, and where they placed their concerns—were not being affected by their membership in the Church.

If they were concerned for civil rights, they had held that concern before they came to the Church. If they were concerned about ministry to the sick, that concern had been prior to church membership and had likely led them to us. Those who held conservative social positions did not relate those convictions to Christian faith at all. For them, Christian faith was in another compartment of life.

During the period after leaving that parish, I had, as I said, time to reflect upon my experience. My values had been formed by my faith; indeed, many had been changed by my faith. My childhood formation in society had been challenged by, reshaped by, the scriptures and doctrines of the Church. I heard the scriptures speaking to me about my life and moving me to ministry. I asked myself, "What happened to me which caused my values, my understanding of myself and the world, to be conditioned by Christianity? They weren't always, I know, but what happened to me?" In the midst of this reflection, as I read an essay by Aidan Kavanagh, one phrase caught my attention: ". . . *catechesis* begins to appear more as a matter of conversion therapy than an exercise in 'religious education.' "[1] As I

---

[1] Aidan Kavanagh. "Christian Initiation: Tactics and Strategy." *Made, Not Born*. (Notre Dame, IN: University of Notre Dame Press, 1976), page 4.

MICHAEL W. MERRIMAN

read Kavanagh's paper I began to realize what had happened to me, what had formed me.

For a number of years I had been attracted toward a new way of life and had come to believe that it would be, when achieved, the most important event in my life. To get to that goal I had to do some investigation, talking to others already living that life, being examined by them, and finally being approved to join a larger number of people also pursuing that goal. For three years I learned to know the scriptures. I learned a new vocabulary. I learned a new way of thinking and acting, and began to look towards a time when I would be made different. Eventually I was admitted to be a candidate for my goal and was examined even more closely by those who were already part of that life, especially by bishops and presbyters. Finally came the moment which I thought at the time was the most important moment in my life. I was ordained.

As I studied the catechumenate, it struck me that the ordination process in the Episcopal Church is essentially a catechumenal process. If non-ordained Christians were to be formed in Christian living, some such process would be needed for them as well.

Then I went back to parish ministry.

My new parish was on the verge of growth and was ready for change. My congregation wanted to grow and extend its ministry in the community. I began to talk to them and teach them about Baptism. I also kept my eye out for a possible baptismal candidate. We found one. (They are not that hard to find, it just depends on where you go. They don't show up at church very often for one thing, and they're hard for the clergy to find because they can see us coming.)

Our first catechumen was brought into the parish by an active member who was dating her (they're now married

Formation in Social Justice and Ministry

and he was recently ordained). When I found that she wished to be baptized, I set out to get the parish involved. We asked her after a time to choose some people in the congregation to be her sponsors. In the meantime we had a small house church group which included her fiance, and I discussed the catechumenate with them and invited them to share in it. We met weekly for a supper and shared the scriptures from the preceding Sunday together.

We did many things in this group which I now know better than to do. It was directed by me far too much, for one thing, and it did not include the larger parish early on. But there were few directions available back in 1978. I had read all I could find, especially by Aidan Kavanagh and Ralph Kiefer, but they didn't give us a program and, in fact, insisted that the catechumenate is not a program. We did have the draft rites for the Catechumenate which were being prepared for *The Book of Occasional Services,* but otherwise we had to make up what we were doing. We were lucky in that, I think.

As we reflected upon the Sunday scriptures, I found that none of the group had an overall understanding of salvation history, so I began to teach its content to them and we would read the passages in that light. Our reflections on the scriptures seemed always to focus on prayer, worship, and ministry, and particular issues of justice in our local community and in the larger world came up again and again.

I must add here that I thought of the components of prayer and worship, but I didn't expect social justice to come up. One of the issues brought to our attention (I seem to remember that it was Paula, the catechumen, who brought it up) was a conflict in our community over the proposed opening of a half-way house for mentally retarded adults. It was being opposed by a number of powerful people in the community. Our concern was taken to the local ministerial council and the churches in the community were able to give the support the project needed to overcome the opposition.

That catechumen, like the ones I have known since, was already teaching the Church even though she wasn't baptized. She was the catalyst which caused all of us in the group to grow. Her catechumenal experience caused the entire parish to be aware of Baptism as it had never been before. Its Lenten program was focused on the catechumen's preparation. Our Easter Vigil had to be reshaped (and our Episcopalian image of the baptismal rite) because she asked to be immersed. We had to secure a large trough, too large to be placed in the building, and do the baptism in the church yard. Just that factor caused a number of people to be involved rather than the small number it takes to do the logistics for the usual baptism (moving the trough, decorating it, securing a source of hundreds of gallons of warm water in the church yard, moving the entire congregation out of the church and back during the vigil, and getting her dried off and into a white robe).

In the next years in that parish we had several other catechumens and we learned better ways to do the catechumenate. But the basic learning came with the first.

I want to share with you what we learned.

Our first discovery was that ministry, prayer, and worship begin with conversion, not with initiation. We learned that the ministry of people is already in them, not something given to them after Baptism. It begins to open up in them as soon as they begin to convert. We learned what, if we had paid attention to Christian theology, we would have known already—that God's grace is operative in human beings before they ever know God. Grace is truly prevenient. There is not a point at which a person begins to catch grace.

Formation in Social Justice and Ministry

We began to find that the first step is to ask people this: "What brought you here?" Often they would stumble over the question because what brought them there seemed to have nothing to do with religion. They would try to define some spiritual experience which often was not the real reason. But then they would begin to define something which seemed non-spiritual. They came out of curiosity. Their car broke down and they came into the church building to ask for help during a weekday Eucharist and the service and the warmth of the people called them back. They worked with members of the parish on secular community projects and something about our attitude toward the life of the community attracted them. Others came because the building looked interesting or beautiful.

We began to help them redefine such moments as in fact the action of God's own leading: that the Holy Spirit can work anywhere and in any way.

Another important discovery was that we needed each other if our concerns for human needs were to move into action. As individuals we might be concerned and we might do some thing about that concern, but it was when we were in a group who shared the scriptures and prayed together that we found ourselves being moved on into action.

We also discovered that our worship in the liturgy began to be transformed as we brought into it our experience of actual, active involvement, in concrete works of love rather than vague good intentions. This was defined for me in a discussion about the liturgy one day when someone asked why we spoke of "the Prayers of the People" if it was a deacon who said them. As I explained that in fact all the deacon does is announce subjects for prayer and the people do the praying, we began to see those prayers as announcing the agenda for ministry in the coming week, and reporting on the ministry we had been en-

MICHAEL W. MERRIMAN

gaged in as a community in the previous week. One of the catechumens pointed out that it seems meaningless to say, "Lord, have mercy," when the deacon says, "Let us pray for the poor," if we do not commit ourselves to active ministry for the poor. If we respond to the call to pray for peace and justice, we must be committed to peace and justice among ourselves and to work for it in the world.

The best thing that happened in that parish was that as the newly converting members become enthused with their lives of service and prayer, and with their discovery of salvation history as the story of their lives, they begin luring the already baptized members into the same enthusiasm. We would point out to them that they were, in fact, being used: used by God and by the community to call all of us back to our baptismal commitment.

That is why, in the Patristic Church, the catechumens were an order of ministry. They have a specific ministry above all to image the continual process of conversion from the world's conventions into Christ which is at the heart of all Christian living. It is one of the most important of all the orders of ministry. It's why they are "ordained" or set apart at the beginning of the catechumenate by being signed with the cross. It is why they should be prayed for as a group like the presbyters and deacons.

Another discovery came. The congregation began finding baptismal candidates. I was relieved of that responsibility because they were better at it. A related discovery was that, as a busy parish priest, it was very difficult to run the catechumenal program myself. I had to depend on the laity. It was hard at first to believe that lay persons could be trusted with the formation of new Christians. It became obvious, however, that it is not the catechist who forms people: it is the Holy Spirit who forms Christians.

This last was the greatest discovery of the catechume-

Formation in Social Justice and Ministry

nate. What we're doing is taking seriously the Holy Spirit as the active agent in bringing about faith and conversion. We are taking our own dogma seriously. This is of course particularly hard for clergy because we work so hard at doing it ourselves; we're sure that the Holy Spirit can't get anything done without us.

The learning goes on.

Now, here at Grace Cathedral, we are still struggling with doing the catechumenate in a very different sort of setting. We have found that in the process of reflecting upon our experience of prayer, worship, and ministry in the light of the scriptures, that there are many people in the congregation, baptized and unbaptized, who are models for Christian living. Our prior concern in formation programs for covering all the bases in a school model of various subjects—Bible, doctrine, worship, etc.—is accomplished in this much less structured sharing by numbers of believers. Best of all, those involved are being led into active forms of ministry for justice and reconciliation in the world.

In this cathedral's congregation I find that a very large proportion of those involved in its outreach program are people who were involved first in the catechumenate and people in our parallel process of formation for confirmation, reception, or reaffirmation. They became involved in, and often were the initiators of, the various ministries while they were still in formation, while they were still unbaptized or unconfirmed. They became involved in the very early stages of their journey or, in some cases, were already involved in secular forms of ministry and helped the Church become involved too.

There was a group preparing for Confirmation last year. As the members of the group were telling their personal stories as part of salvation history, one of the men in his story revealed that he had AIDS. The sharing of his story

MICHAEL W. MERRIMAN

led to the formation of the cathedral's AIDS ministry. Those who lead this ministry were in most cases new members of the congregation. They didn't ask the cathedral to form an AIDS ministry, they formed one. They didn't turn to the clergy to do it, they did it themselves.

This is what we mean by formation.

I am very concerned lest the Church develop a national office for the catechumenate with curricula and programs and systems, timed to the calendar and assuming that Christians are formed according to schedule. I fear that we will institutionalize the catechumenate into a passing fad. What I suspect will happen instead, however, is that as congregations develop the catechumenate, they (and the larger Church) will discover that conversion and formation cannot be programmed—that the catechumens in the power of the Holy Spirit will break structured programs apart.

Robert Hovda has written:

> Eventually, a Church that does something about a regular initiation catechesis experience for its members every Lent and Easter finds that it does have the means to be a "reflective body with regard to issues of import outside the church door." It will no longer be in the position of merely exhorting its individual members to take private positions on political, economic, and other social questions. Its common prayer will bring it together and its common faith will lead it to preach the good news to the poor, to proclaim liberty to captives and new sight to the blind. It will speak to social questions as a community respecting the limits of its competence but with the boldness of faith and the Spirit.[2]

---

[2]Robert Hovda. "Hope for the Future: A Summary." *Made, Not Born.* (Notre Dame, IN: University of Notre Dame Press, 1976), page 160.

Earlier in this conference someone asked Richard Norris whether social justice issues were outside the competence of the Church. I have learned from the catechumenate that if the Church is to be an alternative society, the society of those who assist Christ in serving the world and bringing the kingdom to be, then the place where we begin our social justice agenda is within the Church. We cannot, for example, preach to the world about the rights of women in our society as long as we have not dealt with the rights of women in the Church. If male clergy in a male-dominated Church stand up and preach to the world about its treatment of women, the world has every right to came back and say, "What are you talking about? Look what you do." We cannot lecture the world about peace and reconciliation in Central America or in the cities of our own society if we are not building within the Church a community in which there is peace and reconciliation. I really think this is true and not an attempt to avoid dealing with those issues in the larger society. I am speaking of a Church which finds itself actually competent to address these issues, and we are not competent if we are not a community in which social justice is visible.

If the world sees us as a community in which its own members are being fed, then we can give the world an image of feeding the hungry which will be an example. (We don't even feed our people decently at the heavenly banquet. We give them fake bread and a sip of wine.) We have to be unashamed of who we are in the world—a group of people who started off as an outlawed sect running a soup kitchen.

We have to rediscover that when a small group of people who have been captured by the Spirit of God share in prayer and in worship the story of salvation and begin reflecting on their own experience as part of that story, their whole picture of the world and of themselves is turned upside down and they become different people. When that happens publicly in the view of the community of the faithful, the community either turns it off because it is too threatening or it gets hooked and begins to be converted.

It seems to me, as I said earlier, that it is the right wing churches that are forming their people to live with conviction in the world. Meanwhile the "liberal" churches keep assuming that an unthought-out programmatic approach based on religious education will somehow produce people who at least "won't do nothin' and won't hurt nobody."

When was the last time the Episcopal Church had any real influence on American Society? In spite of our attempts to pressure US businesses out of South Africa, we had no success. (Some have left, but only because it was becoming economically uncertain. IBM did not pull out because of pressure from the General Convention.) Other than the black churches (which know how to form people in a common story), no churches can take much credit for the successes of the civil rights movement.

But there is hope for something new for those who share in catechumenal gatherings. For example, on the Second Sunday of Advent our catechumens were discussing the readings they had just heard in the liturgy. They had heard the words from Isaiah, "Comfort ye my people . . . he will feed his flock like a shepherd." They began their reflection. One person who had AIDS shared his experience of being cared for and of then finding that the best care was his involvement in caring for others who have AIDS. Another person shared the work that she had gotten involved with at a sanctuary for the homeless. What I had thought would be a discussion from the Gospel of the day about John the Baptist and about Baptism instead became a discussion about ways our congregation can more effectively minister to the sick and dying and to the homeless.

On the First Sunday after the Epiphany the group found again the Old Testament reading to be directing their reflection: "I have given you as a covenant to the people, a light to the nations to open the eyes that are blind and to bring out prisoners from the dungeon." One person brought up the fact that a group from Grace Cathedral was going to Nicaragua, and they began talking about peace in Central America and the need to work for peace in our society and within the Church. (In catechumenal groups the issue of the lack of peace and reconciliation within the Church often comes up. Early on I was afraid to let new Christians find out that Christians don't get along with each other. "Let's get them in first; they will find out soon enough." But this doesn't work with the catechumenate. They see the Church, warts and all, and that is good. It is good because it cuts out from the beginning any chance of their conversion into faith in God being sidetracked into conversion to faith in an ecclesiastical institution.)

The discoveries we have made by doing the catechumenate, then, are the following. First, the ministry of Christians for peace, justice, and reconciliation begins at conversion, not after initiation. Secondly, we need each other to move beyond concern into action. Third, our worship in the liturgy is transformed and made alive as we bring into it the experience of active involvement in concrete works of love, rather than simply bringing in our own vague good intentions. And fourth, as these newly converting members become enthused with their ministries, they lure the older members into action as well and begin to transform the community.

Robert Brooks has written these words on this subject:

Baptism is the source of "re-membering." It tells us

"who we are and who we are becoming," as John the Deacon wrote in the year 500. It tells us that we are the Christ, daily being made more and more into his image. This is dangerous and subversive information. Those who regard human life as worth little are able to countenance any sort of social injustice. Those who know themselves as images of God have a profound sense of dignity and worth born of knowing their divine heritage; and, aware that every other person is also the Christ, they are not satisfied until economic and social structures provide dignity and care for all.

The Early Church's baptismal liturgy was an experience of social justice, of a new social order, the reign of God. By modeling a new social order, a new creation, in the catechumenate and in baptism, the early church subverted the Roman Empire from within rather than challenging it head on . . . Christians proclaimed in word and deed that only Jesus, who had accomplished their liberation by his death and resurrection, was the Lord. This undercut allegiance to the Roman imperial system. It is no wonder the Roman Empire persecuted the Christian community . . .

By choosing voluntarily to forego food, the faithful have made themselves powerless, too. They are ready to stand with the "marginal" of their own community, those called to baptism this Easter. They are thus prepared to discover that, contrary to our society's wisdom, sharing their goods does not deprive them of worth or being; rather, it enables them to be filled with the sense of wholeness and "new creation" that is the heart of the Easter Vigil. This is what the Fathers called "festive fasting." When we choose to be dispossessed of material good, we rediscover it as sacramental; we learn that it is meant to lead us to relationship, not to be an end in itself . . .

Formation in Social Justice and Ministry

Adult baptism at the Easter Vigil shows the world how God sees the human race. As Nathan Mitchell has noted, the experience of a catechumen in baptism is radically in contrast with the usual experience of interaction in daily life. Where else does one experience being lovingly bathed, massaged with perfumed oil, clothed in a beautiful new garment, embraced, fed, incensed? Yet these are true symbols of the way God sees us; as we act out this love at the Easter Vigil, we reveal the new humanity that God is working to build . . . Here is a description John Chrysostom gave of a baptismal liturgy at Antioch in the fourth century:

> As soon as the newly baptized come forth from those sacred waters, all who are present embrace them, kiss them, rejoice with them, and congratulate them, because those who were heretofore slaves and captives have suddenly become free men and women and sons and daughters and have been invited to the royal table.[3]

As Augustine of Hippo, teaching the newly baptized about the sacraments in his cathedral on Easter, said:

> You are the body of Christ. In you and through you the work of the incarnation must go forward. You are to be taken, you are to be blessed, broken, and distributed. That you may be the means of grace and the vehicles of the eternal charity.

---

[3] Robert Brooks. "The Great Feast, Font of Justice." *Liturgy: Feasts and Fasting*. The Liturgical Conference, Washington, DC.

MICHAEL W. MERRIMAN

VI

The Role of the Bishop in Christian Initiation

ROGER J. WHITE, *Bishop of Milwaukee*

"What the Church says about who the Catechumens are as they enter the font, is to say what the Church is—it is the source of our ecclesiology." *(Aidan Kavanagah)*

"In the course of their Christian development, those baptized at an early age are expected, when they are ready and have been duly prepared, to make a mature public affirmation of their faith and commitment to the *responsibilities* of their Baptism and to receive the laying on of hands by the bishop." *(From the Rubric of the Confirmation service: taken from the first paragraph of "Concerning the Service.")*

It is my belief that the role of the bishop in Christian initiation is to be a visionary, to be a teacher, to be a supporter "of the ministry of the clergy and laity, as shepherd to be the icon of God", and finally, to be a participant in the planning, implementation and journeying in faith with and for those who seek to make a mature affirmation of their baptismal covenant. If you are to understand the role of the bishop as it relates to Christian initiation, and particularly in the catechumenate process, it may be helpful to have some understanding of my own background and, secondly, some understanding of the process which has been adapted by the Diocese of Milwaukee as it has developed a pilot project for the catechumenate in the Episcopal Church.

My own experience, especially with Baptism and Confirmation, comes from my background both as a member of the Church of England and as a priest in the Church of England. That experience gave me a somewhat jaundiced view of both those initiation rites. My own Confirmation at the early age of eleven left me with little foundation or commitment to the way of Jesus Christ. My experience as a priest in the Church of England developed a strong antagonism to the purely mechanical aspects of baptizing infants and presenting young people for Confirmation with inadequate preparation or understanding of what they or their sponsors were committing themselves to in the life of the Church. My training and background are strong in baptismal theology and a tradition which is Eucharistically centered. My experience in this province of the Anglican Church with rites of initiation did not particularly alter my jaundiced view of our use of the initiation rites of the Church. I have found a lack of preparation of both parents and sponsors for those infants who are to be baptized and, secondly, a method of preparing people for Confirmation or Reception which has been mainly an exchange of information concerning the ways and teachings of the Church. The past methods of preparation for these initiation rites does not lead to an understanding of the faith that we are called to follow, nor to a commitment to our Lord Jesus Christ, nor to an understanding of what our mission and ministry as members of the Body of Christ is to be.

This led me eventually as a parish priest to move away from the conventional methods of preparation for Confirmation for those wishing to be confirmed or received, and to begin to use as a basis for preparation the baptismal covenant. As we began to explore God's encounter of us and our response to that encounter, and its ensuing call to ministry, we found that the sharing of people's faith journeys became an enormously helpful method of understanding both God's intervention in the lives of individuals and their response to that intervention. This gradually developed into a curriculum for adults, and adults only, who wished to reaffirm their baptismal promises and who were willing to share their experiences of God and their hopes for a fruitful ministry as members of the Body of Christ—both to that body and to the world in which they live.

When I became a bishop in the Diocese of Milwaukee I had a conversation with Dr. Wayne Schwab of the Evangelism Department of our National Church, who was seeking a diocese in which to explore the possibilities of a pilot project for the catechumenate. My background and my preparation found me ready to respond positively to that invitation. We began, together with Dr. Schwab's staff and some individuals in our diocese—both clergy and laity—to explore a possible catechumenal process for the Episcopal Church. The development of this process began with a survey of every known parish in the Episcopal Church who had utilized a catechumenate program, and through an intensive survey we were able to gather a multitude of learnings from those parochial experiences. The greatest learning from that survey, I believe, was that most of the catechumenal programs developed in parishes tended to be the pet projects of a particular clergy person. If that person left the parish, often there was no continuity to the program.

The Role of the Bishop in Christian Initiation

It was at this point that we decided that it was very important that a catechumenal process should be a diocesan process which involved strong support of the diocesan bishop. In this way, such a process would have continuity and would hopefully become the process, both for new people coming into the Life of the Church and for people who had been members of the Church for many years, to participate together in a journey of faith leading to a reaffirmation of their baptismal promises—either in the form of Confirmation, Reception or Reaffirmation. As an undergirding preparation for this program, I spent 18 months preaching in my diocese on the baptismal covenant at all parish visitations and on any other opportunity where members of the diocese were gathered. Not only did the baptismal covenant become the focus of preaching, it also became the theological rationale for our diocesan budget, which in the past had been purely a balance sheet or an outline of program. That strong infusion of baptismal covenant theology preached by the bishop became, I believe, the theological basis for our being able to move as a diocese into this particular adaptation of the catechumenal process—which I am about to outline.

It was my hope and my vision that we may as a diocese work toward the goal of developing mature commitment in members of the Church—both those who had been members of the Church for long periods of time and those who were coming into the fellowship of the Church for the first time. I believe that what we do by way of initiation in the Life of the Church is pointed out in the quotation by Aidan Kavanagh; it tells us what our ecclesiology is as a community of faith. *The Book of Occasional Services* defines the catechumenal process as, "a period of training and instruction in Christian understanding of God, human relationships, the meaning of life, and culminates in the reception of sacraments of Christian initiation." We hope that through an adaptation of the traditional understanding of the catechumenate we will be able to produce a deep commitment to the following of our Lord Jesus Christ in the lives of those who make this journey of faith. We hope that this journey of faith leads them to see that their primary witness as newly committed or recommitted Christians is to be in their daily places—in their work, in their community, in their leisure time and in their faith community—people who know God and his ways and respond to that encounter with God, and who live out their faith in their daily living as they proclaim the Gospel in word and deed.

I feel most fortunate that I inherited a diocese whose practice had already been not to present anyone for Confirmation or Reception who was under age 16, and we have continued that practice. The Diocese of Milwaukee only presents adults for Confirmation. This catechumenal process in the life of the Diocese of Milwaukee is called "Living Our Baptismal Covenant." It is an adaptation of the catechumenate process because it also includes those who are already baptized, whereas the catechumenate process is more specifically for the unbaptized. This process does offer a methodology whereby both those who are unbaptized and those who have been baptized as infants and have come to the point of reaffirming their baptismal promises may journey together in preparation for that public commitment and initiation.

We have come to believe that this process is first and foremost about formation as a follower of Christ, and formation for the ministry of those who are baptized and have come to the point of making that mature reaffirmation. The need for such a process has been further endorsed by our learning that 50 percent of adults who are incorporated into the Episcopal Church through traditional Confirmation and

Reception preparation are no longer active after three to four years. It is further endorsed by the learning that those prepared as young teenagers have a low retention rate in the life of the Church. It is believed that only one out of twelve persons prepared as a young teen in the Episcopal Church remains a member of the Church in adult life. It is our hope that this preparation for initiation, which is an intentional preparation of adults for their life and ministry in the world, supported by their life and fellowship in the Church, will reduce this enormous loss of activity and participation in the life of local parishes and the Church as a whole. It is also our hope that it will enable individuals to find their ministry within the Body of Christ, probably more especially in their life in the world.

If Baptism is to be taken seriously, preparation of both parents and sponsors and, later in life, mature Christians who wish to take upon themselves the promises made for them as infants, needs to be an in-depth and serious journey of faith which leads to an active and fruitful ministry. It is my belief that a bishop of a diocese needs to be able to grasp the vision of this journey of faith, to be a willing supporter and participant in the diocesan team which develops the process, to be the "icon of God" as shepherd, concerned and caring enough that the people of his diocese have the opportunity to come to this point of commitment and response to God's action in their lives by being enabled to develop a strong ministry in their parish, in the Church, and in the world.

As this particular process is outlined, you will see that it takes not only a large time commitment and energy commitment on the part of the bishop but also on the part of the laity and the clergy who are supportive of the concept as they develop this particular process on the parish level. It is, in my view, essential that the bishop take seriously the

ROGER J. WHITE

role of teacher, both in preaching and in participation at the parish level in teaching the faith to those who are "committed to this one year journey of faith which we call Living Our Baptismal Covenant" (which is the adaptation of the catechumenal process for the Diocese of Milwaukee and, hopefully in the future, for much of the Episcopal Church).

Let me now turn to the more practical aspects of this catechumenal process as it has been developed in the Diocese of Milwaukee. Working with the National Church staff led by Dr. Wayne Schwab, with Dr. Louis Weil of Nashotah House (a well known liturgical scholar in the Episcopal Church), and with a group of clergy and lay people from the Diocese of Milwaukee, we spent some eighteen months in exploring what form this particular process should take. This involved all of us—bishop, people, and outside staff—in a great amount of reading so that we could have a good understanding of the catechumenate and the rites of initiation as they are understood in the Anglican Church. It meant that we had to spend a considerable amount of time adapting traditional catechumenal processes to our particular needs, and involved participation in a workshop of the Roman Catholic Church.

At the end of that long period of working together and preparation, we came up with a basic design and decided to choose five parishes in the Diocese of Milwaukee to be the five pilot parishes for the first year-long journey of faith. From these five parishes, laity and clergy formed parish teams who were in turn trained by the diocesan team, supported by the National Church staff. We also recognized that much of the learning for these teams would take place in the actual situations within their parishes as they journeyed for the first time. We had an outline of the process, but it also became very obvious to us that that outline would be adapted by the local parish and would look quite different in the five parishes who participated in this initial pilot process. Different methodologies were used and leadership in some parishes was by the laity, in others by the clergy. The process followed a basic pattern but was indeed different in each of the five parishes.

That basic outline of the process is as follows. In the late summer and early fall there is a process of *gathering*. This particular process can involve parish evangelism committees; it can involve the catechumenal team in not only identifying people within the congregation to be invited, but also inviting new people in the life of the parish to participate in this process.

The next stage, which begins in the fall, is a period of *inquiry* in which the faith of the Church is shared with the individuals and they pursue their inquiry about the faith as it is interpreted and taught by the Episcopal Church. This second phase is also an opportunity for people to discover within the group whether they wish to inquire further and pursue this journey of faith in more intensity.

If they so choose to pursue this during the pre-Lenten and Lenten season, there is a phase of *intensive formation* in Christ which is a sharing of faith journeys, both by the participants and the team, and by the bishop of the diocese and others from the Church who are invited to share their own personal journey of faith. This *intensive formation* also involves a strong biblical undergirding as part of formation in Christ, the "bursting open of the word of God."

The fourth phase is during Holy Week and is preparation for the rites of initiation and the renewal of our baptismal covenant on Holy Saturday. In many of our parishes this involved a day of retreat, or in some parishes an overnight retreat. It involved a full participation in the liturgy of Holy Week, which led to a climax either for Baptism on

Holy Saturday or the reaffirmation of baptismal promises. This particular week is an intensive week of journeying with this particular community, and joining the whole parish community in the liturgy of that week. It is a time for strong community building on the part of those who are making this journey.

Easter Week is the time when the bishop holds two regional Confirmations and Receptions. At that time, in both the eastern part of the diocese and in the western part of the diocese, the bishop meets with the candidates for Confirmation, Reception, and Reaffirmation, and spends some three to four hours meeting with them prior to the service—as teacher, as sharer of his faith journey, of being very much present as shepherd in that particular small community which has journeyed together in faith. The post-Easter phase is one of the most important but also one of the most difficult. It is in the whole area of mystagogia—it is that important time when we give those making the journey of faith the opportunity to experience ministry and to discern their own particular gifts and adapt those gifts to a particular ministry in the Life of the Church. It is also critically important that they develop a goodly understanding of what their ministry is as a follower of Christ in their own particular place in this world where God has placed them, so that they may exercise their ministry in all of their living. The temptation is to peak at Easter and ignore this critical integration phase in the post-Easter Season. This five stage process of gathering, inquiry, intensive formation, journeying through Holy Week, and the celebration and formal public reaffirmation of their baptismal covenant, followed by an understanding and experience of ministry, forms the basic outline of this catechumenal process. The role of the bishop, I believe, is to be a part of the planning team, a participant at the parish level in the process, a focus of teaching during both Holy Week and Easter Week, and a continual supporter and source of enthusiasm throughout the process.

I am not going to detail the particulars of these five important phases. Rather, I would prefer to share with you what has happened since that first year when five parishes led that process and experiment. We had decided that the commitment involved generated a tremendous amount of enthusiasm on the part of the team and the participants. We had a very, very small dropout rate, both at the team and at the participant level, although a considerable amount of time was demanded from both. Some parishes have worked this into their Sunday morning schedule and some have offered this as a Sunday afternoon or evening process. Others have met during the week—it has varied enormously from parish to parish depending on their parish schedule and the availability of the participants. We decided that we could not burden those five parishes with the responsibility of sharing the process with new parishes who wished to be a part of the process. We therefore formed a catechumenal Transition Team in the diocese. It is made up of priests, permanent deacons, and lay people who have been trained to work with new parish teams who wish to join in this process.

We had ten parishes in our diocese who indicated an interest in joining as new parishes in this process and we chose six this year. Those six parishes have begun their training with a three day long training session for their parish teams which has been enthusiastically received. They feel as though they are well on their way to preparing for the beginning of that particular process in the fall of 1988. The Transitional Team will continue to work with each of those parish teams as they prepare to enter this process.

In the meantime, the five original parishes are now

ROGER J. WHITE

halfway through their second year. They have made some adaptation of their own particular processes, but they are finding great success and enthusiasm in the second year of the program. This will mean that by the fall of 1988, the Diocese of Milwaukee will have 20% of its parishes enrolled in this process. We already have a waiting list of parishes who wish to begin the training of their parish teams in the early part of 1989.

Let me briefly talk about the aspects of commitment involved. For most of our parish teams, this involves beginning in August and working almost through to the following July. For participants it usually means that they begin the process in September and go through the end of June each year. The regular commitment is an average of one meeting per week; at certain stages of the process it sometimes involves a commitment of two and a half hours per week. We have not found any difficulty in having both the teams and the participants make this commitment once they have begun this process. The coordinator of our particular program is a parish priest, who is aided for administrative purposes by a seminary-trained permanent deacon, whose role is growing as the number of parishes participating increases. We also are finding ourselves being called upon to share this particular program with other dioceses who have learned of this pilot project through a variety of publications and articles which have been written and distributed. It is anticipated that this spring the Department of Evangelism of the Episcopal Church will publish this process for distribution in the Episcopal Church, which will enable other dioceses to grasp the concept and begin moving toward the development of their own catechumenal process for preparing those who are to be initiated or who are to reaffirm their baptismal promises.

It is my hope as the bishop of this particular diocese that

this process will help to build up the Church, to develop strong and committed followers of Christ who will have high participation in a variety of ministries and a much better understanding of what Christ's call entails as we live out our faith in our daily places. I believe that it is essential that the body be built up in order that it may respond to God's actions in our lives and then in turn reach out in love, caring, and ministry to all people in this world as we attempt to be like our Lord Jesus Christ—people for others.

This particular methodology which we have chosen does incorporate a strong emphasis on evangelism, as we gather people together to participate in this program. It takes seriously the rubric for Confirmation, where we ask people who are mature and who are indeed ready and duly prepared to make that public affirmation of their faith—a commitment to the responsibilities of their Baptism as they receive the laying on of hands by a bishop of the Church. It is my belief that we already are beginning to see an enthusiasm to proclaim the Gospel both by word and by example—a much clearer understanding of what God's call implies by way of living out our faith in our daily ministry as we try, as members of the body, to seek and serve Christ in all—to strive for justice and peace, respecting the dignity of every human being.

It is my sincere hope that this process will enable us to stop spinning our wheels with "Confirmation preparation" as we have known it in the past and to offer an in-depth spiritual journey, that many who seek a close knowledge of God and his ways will be able to find within the Life of the Church, and provide the opportunity for that encounter. It is also my hope that they will begin to see the fruits of that encounter as they respond with committed ministries.

I also believe that this is an opportunity for the Church to be truly involved in mutual ministry. In many of the parishes, the catechumenate teams are now led by lay people and the clergy of the parish are there to support and to be resources for those teams. This sharing of ministry enables a continued development of an understanding of the ministry of the baptized—both those who are in Orders and those who are not. It is a commitment by both priest and people to a "flesh and blood" experience of the Church.

This process avoids the temptation to indoctrinate people with the priest's favorite and often abstract theology of the Church, or with obscure historical aspects of its past life. It is about bringing those who wish to journey with Christ up-close to the life of the community, "warts" and all. It is a commitment to be incarnational in our life and in our ministry. This process calls upon the bishop to have some flexibility concerning visitation and Confirmation rounds. If, indeed, we get to the stage where many Confirmations take place in Easter week, the bishop's visitation to the parish becomes a visitation in which he can be seen as chief celebrant and as chief presider of the Eucharist, and as teacher of the people and allowed to spend extended time with the people of the parish, rather than going to the parish "for Confirmation." This means that a bishop has to have a strong commitment to setting aside Holy Week and Easter Week to be with the people, and also to be flexible to look at new ways of utilizing the opportunity to visit parishes in the diocese.

This catechumenal process developed in the Diocese of Milwaukee is an intentional attempt at systemic change as we form people in the faith. That formation, I believe, is critical for the future of the Episcopal Church as we live our faith in the midst of a secular society. The overall role of the bishop is to be the shepherd of the people in his care; that involves proclaiming the Gospel of Jesus Christ, that others may respond to that salvation news. That is the task

The Role of the Bishop in Christian Initiation

of the baptised, and the bishop needs to witness to that ministry in his own life, in the design of the ministry of the diocese, and for the future growth and welfare of the Church.

The bishop must grasp the vision and work diligently to teach, support and participate in the process, because our forming of people in the faith is the essence of what the Church is called to be in this world—a people formed in Christ to be the witness to the Gospel in both their words and their deeds, as they seek Christ in serving all people and strive for justice and peace.

ROGER J. WHITE

… VII.

The Catechumenate and Christian Formation of the Parish Community

WALTER L. GUETTSCHE

"How can this young woman live in the real world after all this?!"

This question asked by a skeptical critic of the adult catechumenate as we completed the final days before Vicky's baptism in Emmanuel parish, Houston, is really the question asked of all of us. What is it to live in the "real" world following formation into a community rooted in faith and life in Christ? This is our challenge to authenticity!

Probably the question being raised concerns a perception that Christian faith and lifestyle differ little from the values of the secular world. (Are we forming "misfits," persons unfit for society?) The threat of the catechumenate is that it might ask more of all of us—maybe even conversion or transformation—change, risk, authenticity, wholeness, perception of Christian faith and lifestyle in *all* facets of our life. The transformation of which we speak is, as the

New Testament sees it, of turning around in another direction following a new life: life in Christ.

Is there really any discernible lifestyle difference in our parishes in which we live, or are they merely reflections of the "world"? Is it not the case that the real crisis facing Christian Initiation is baptism into unformed community?

1. A Post-Constantinian World Greets The Episcopal Church

In January, 1972, Massey H. Shepherd, Jr. wrote an article ("Confirmation: The Early Church" in *Worship* magazine) in which he heralded the "post-Constantinian era" while proclaiming the "Paschal Mystery" as singular sacrament in the experience of the Early Church.

> The nurture and education of baptized children in Christian families in a Christian society were pastoral concerns of discipline intended to make them responsible communicants in a church coterminous with the nation. Today this ideal is a romantic fiction, as our Western society becomes increasingly secularized. We live in a post-Constantinian, if not a pre-Constantinian era, when Christian communities and congregations must accept again in a pluralistic society a status of voluntary groups without special privilege or support from society generally. We may not be persecuted as in the early centuries before Constantine, but possibly we suffer a worse fate from society as a whole by its indifference. And this indifference is compounded by the larger number of nominal and uncommitted Christians on our church rolls.[1]

---

[1] Massey H. Shepherd, "Confirmation: The Early Church," *Worship,* Volume 46, Number 1, January 1972, pp. 19–20.

His point is appropriate to our consideration that many continue to believe that the Church and the world are synonymous, in a presumption that we live in an inherently Christian society, on the one hand, or that the Church should not require too much of us or confuse us with a conflict in values with the secular world in which we live, on the other.

What is the alternative? Is it the rise of fundamentalism, with its characteristic attitude of "critical parent" attempting to recover the unity of an institutionalized Christianity, with the Church as "watchdog" of the societal morality? For us in the Catholic tradition, there must be alternatives, and I believe there are.

Experience with the adult catechumenate in two very different parishes offers encouragement to the questions raised regarding Church and society, formation in faith and lifestyle versus desperation of some to recover a powerful place in society by judgment and coercion (or by the rise of media consumer "quick-fix" fundamentalist renewal).

What is it to be a Christian in the "world"? How might our parish communities form us to live effectively in day to day life? How might parish communities themselves be more effective in relating in and to the "world" (through evangelization and mission—speaking and action in morality and justice)?

THE TEXAS ENVIRONMENT

Texas developmentally functions as a "third coast" characterized, especially in Houston and Dallas, by urbanization and transient population—secular and detached. The potential for unbaptized adults is greater in such an environment. (Although, I do not discount the fact that small towns may be just as vulnerable to the agnostic spirit in relation to establishment churches.) In transition from the apparent

Christianity of the Southern Baptist cultural dominance (still alive), there is, nevertheless a general "post-Constantinian" secular population. Our experience with second generation adults from agnostic home backgrounds is that they often have no hostility toward the Church, they simply do not know what we "are about." In other cases, we have those who have had bad experiences in fundamentalist churches who need to work through these judgmental and destructive perceptions and images to a grace-centered spirituality.

2. *Some Pastoral History*

My first encounter with the catechumenate came in 1977, through my friendship with The Reverend Robert J. Brooks who was then Vicar of All Saints' Church, Baytown, Texas (suburb of Houston). While I had completed my academic degree in liturgy and knew of the historical catechumenate, I had never dreamed that it might actually become a reality and would so profoundly affect the life of the parishes where I was to become rector.

The Episcopal Church should be most grateful to Father Brooks and to the All Saints' community of that time. In my perspective as a continuing friend of Garey Atkinson, first catechumen at All Saints', I can only say that he embodies all that we are saying about transformation and formation in faith and lifestyle.

In the fall of 1978, I became Rector of Grace Church, Galveston, an island city off the Texas coast—an historical parish in an inner city, urban environment, with a large Victorian gothic building and a highly pluralistic congregation. In the midst of this over powering museum-like building (a national and state historical site), a small congregation, and the inner city problems of economic struggle and various life sagas, an unbaptized young woman named Melody appeared in 1981, only recently married to one of the parishioners in a civil ceremony. A few weeks later, a young man moved to Galveston named Billy, who came to Grace Church and, after a short time in community, announced that he wanted to become part of the life of the Church. Then John, soon to be married in Los Angeles to an Episcopalian, appeared seeking to become part of the Church through Baptism, hopefully before the marriage. All three were admitted as catechumens, first Melody, then Billy and John. In this small parish—warm and loving, occasionally fixed in time—a smoldering revolution in renewal was in process. The manifestations were stormy at times, but the lives of many will never be the same.

Only a few weeks ago, one of the sponsors of Melody, Nancy Howell, reflected, "When a parish is ready, God's grace will provide the catechumens." Apparently, we were ready.

In the fall of 1983, I became rector of an affluent, suburban parish in Houston of about 500—homogenous at that time, rapidly growing in numbers, and basking in the success of the oil-based economy. Emmanuel parish, Houston—internally in sadness and grief over the untimely early death of my predecessor, mixed with its outwardly stylish, self-contained energy—was like having a "tiger by the tail" for me. I was not sure what might work here, but was certain of the "calling."

The roots of what was to happen were clearly found within the Search Committee for rector. In particular, the Director of Religious Education, Irene Gallaher, already had in mind the integration of catechesis and liturgy. The present Junior Warden, Tim Wade, and the Altar Guild Directress of that time, Trish Roberts, shared in this vision. In addition, the many individuals within this parish, with vision and great love and compassion for the life of the Church and for humanity, embodied in themselves a renewal in Christian Initiation "waiting to happen."

In June of 1984, a young woman named Vicky came to see me, who had visited first on Easter with her mother. Vicky Tickell had been invited to Emmanuel by a business friend, Jerry Christopher, who later became one of her sponsors. In the midst of this somewhat sterile parish environment, Vicky was admitted as a catechumen. In a congregation where some were accustomed to wearing their "church faces and church clothes" with reality safely tucked away in the recesses of each private life, a new vision for the Church as community and its ministry invaded this "safety."

As the catechumenate evolved, we realized that something was happening to all of us. Her presence was a catalyst for authenticity on my part and for the sponsors. Her sponsors consisted of Wanda Slayton, wife of the Senior Warden that year; Paula Martin, the succeeding Senior Warden; and Jerry, the vestry member who brought her to community. Irene, the Director of Religious Education, was vitally involved in how our perception of catechesis and liturgy were evolving.

In the midst of this overwhelming conversion for Vicky and for the parish leadership, the issue of mode of Baptism was raised as a question. Vicky said that only immersion baptism would suffice as symbol to match all that was happening in her life. Pouring was "not nearly enough water" (in her own words) to match the transformation. With much fear and trembling, I approved it with thoughts of how negatively this had been received in Galveston. Then I remembered all the transforming life stories there. One woman had said, "I can never stand for the Eucharistic Prayer or for Communion; I hope you will understand." I

WALTER L. GUETTSCHE

said that I did, but explained the perception of corporate prayer and symbol of resurrection inherent in standing. On Easter morning at the Great Vigil, on seeing the candidates rising from the waters of the font, this same woman stood for Communion and has ever since, so far as I know.

Vicky and Jon, our organist choirmaster, went to Galveston in a truck to get the font a few days before Holy Week. Several parishioners, some most unlikely, refinished the font inside and outside to prepare it for the "formal" space of Emmanuel Church. Meanwhile, in Adult Forum, the congregation studied the Early Church documents and the Prayer Book rubrical history on water baptism by immersion in preparation for the Vigil.

As we anticipated the Great Vigil—the power of water, of light, sound, and vision—the power of resurrection became all the more powerful as we experienced together the scrutinies on the Third, Fourth, and Fifth Sundays in Lent. The catechumenate reflected together on the lessons of the Great Vigil of Easter. In the course of this, Vicky selected the readings. It was at that time that I realized how much had been internalized. I had projected my own vision into the catechetical session that her choice would be one of the great stories from the Pentateuch. Vicky chose the reading from Zephaniah as her favorite, "Sing aloud, O daughter of Zion; shout, O Israel! Rejoice and exult with all your heart, O daughter of Jerusalem! . . . ."[2]

Somehow in the midst of Vicky's baptism, the parish was in preparation for the economic demise of the affluent Memorial area of Houston in the energy crisis. Living the Paschal Mystery became profoundly real as people became real, authentic, and were becoming the "Church."

---

[2] Revised Standard Version.

By the time Jennifer Haley and Christine Howard were admitted as catechumens in 1985, even peripheral parishioners were taking notice that living out our Baptism is foundational to our life. During the Candidacy for Baptism of Jennifer and Christine, the whole congregation gathered on Wednesday nights in Lent to study the lessons in the series called *From Ashes to Easter*.[3]

During the week of the story of the Samaritan woman at the well (the Third Sunday in Lent), we took a surprise field trip to the great cascade of water at the Transco Tower in Houston. There on the lawn, gathered in a circle with the power of water most visible and audible and the great beacon of light from the building, we explored the story. The woman's phrase resounded, "Where do you get that living water?"[4] As our consciousness was raised concerning the power of water in this story involving a Samaritan woman, a stranger kept popping into our group periodically in great curiosity! Returning to the church by the time *Ashes to Easter* groups were completed, the whole congregation gathered in a circle as we concluded with prayers and the *missa* of the catechumenate (laying on of hands and prayer led by the catechist). (In this context on these Wednesday nights, the giving of the Creeds and the Lord's Prayer occurred in the presence of the congregation.) Thereby the integrity of the catechumenate was maintained in small group, but the whole congregation experienced the power of these final days before Baptism.

---

[3]The Liturgical Conference, Washington, D.C., 1979—The rubrical requirement was obeyed that the customary lectionary cycle be maintained, so the congregation studied the appointed Sunday lessons even though the small catechumenate sessions included touch with these classical lessons from the "A" cycle for the scrutinies.

[4]Revised Standard Version.

WALTER L. GUETTSCHE

We have failed in some aspects of the catechumenate and we are learning. One catechumen became a Unitarian because she cannot embrace the Christ symbol, but she was absolutely faithful in her catechumenate, wrote several pages of heart-warming response before I came here to San Francisco, and still appears in our pews on occasion. Another catechumen has dropped out. We failed to engage in a lengthy precatechumenate in our exuberance from previous experience and now understand how important this is.

Now we have admitted Marge Taylor on January 10, 1988, who experienced a lengthy precatechumenate. The admission became very powerful as a consequence. In the midst of tears, she said, "I feel so special."

Physical changes often occur as well as spiritual transformation. We notice, for example, that the catechumen will often enter community by sitting in the back of the Nave or on the far side. As time progresses, the catechumen moves into the "heart" of the congregation, literally. Changes in countenance and physical appearance are often discernible as the persons come to feel good about themselves.

The families of all these people have been profoundly touched. Vicky's mother has become the Co-Directress of the Altar Guild. Her father, a Southern Baptist, made the Good Friday cross to be carried in the liturgy on that day just before his daughter's baptism. Christine's parents are in catechesis currently preparing for Confirmation.

Is it really the case that the presence of one person—of Melody in Grace Church, Galveston, or of Vicky in Emmanuel Church, Houston, is an opening to such dramatic change? We believe that the answer is yes.

Their presence calls us to rethink our whole perception of catechesis and formation; of liturgical community, sacrament, and spirituality; of ministry, mission, and evangeliza-

Christian Formation of the Parish Community

tion; of faith and lifestyle. The catechumen is a gift to parish life.

3. How Might We Identify This Re-formation/Transformation in Parish Life Rooted in Christian Tradition?

WORDS: "FORMATION"—"TRANSFORMATION"

Our use of words can be revelatory. A simple search through a dictionary reveals that "formation" means "an act of giving form or shape to something or of taking form: development."[5] "Form" usually "suggests reference to both internal structure and external outline and often the principle that gives unity to the whole." In light of this, we might reflect by saying that a person or community "formed" or "shaped" begins to assume a discernible external whole (in action) as internalization occurs. The reverse is also true. External action and an external environment also "forms" and "shapes" our deepest internal self, our spirit, our inner core, as well. (This explains the concern in the *Apostolic Tradition* of Hippolytus that certain occupations and roles in the Roman Empire were in conflict "to the formation of Christians in the catechumenate.)[6] Trans" added to "formation" suggests "across, beyond, through, so as to change." Change or conversion often occurs, then, "through" formation—"*trans*formation."

PASTORAL CATECHESIS VERSUS PROGRAM CATECHESIS

Several years ago, I interviewed two pastors of Roman Catholic parishes only a few miles apart. One characterized

---

[5]Quotations from *Webster's Ninth Collegiate Dictionary.*

[6]*Hippolytus: A Text for Students,* trans. and ed. Geoffrey J. Cuming, (Grove Books, 1976), pp. 15–16.

WALTER L. GUETTSCHE

the catechumenate in the parish in terms of time frame, management by the catechesis personnel, "a successful program in which we place candidates." The other pastor warmly described persons, their story, struggle with personal relationship, how the catechesis related to their development, and how he was involved in assessing their readiness for Baptism. I went home and told our Director of Religious Education that I had just heard a story of "program catechesis" in the former, and of "pastoral catechesis" in the latter (thus, I identified these two concepts).

How might we engage in this "pastoral catechesis"? We start where the person is. "Put away all the contrived notebooks, curriculum, lecture notes. Bring out the scripture lectionary and the Prayer Book and be who you are—vulnerable, speaking of your own faith and lifestyle in Christ from your heart and mind."

"Pastoral catechesis" engages us in telling our family story—the story from scripture, in prayer and spirituality, in lifestyle, and in discovering vocation and ministry. The sponsors and the catechists must be willing to share of themselves and to drop the contrived, prepared, sterile "lecturing" we have often called "Christian Education."

Recommended is telling some of the full stories of scripture so that as the lectionary becomes the base for catechesis, the context is perceived. The Passover story, for example, is essential to the full and complete comprehension of much of the Old Testament and certainly of new covenant—in "Christ, our Passover." The stories of scripture, like the stories our grandparents tell us, gives us our identity. (The result of this in the catechumenate is that the long-term Christians begin to want to learn the stories of scripture themselves.)

The catechists do meet and prepare a path. We start with the scripture lectionary, our sense of prayer and spirituality, of the time in which we *are* in liturgical year. The catechumenate convenes and the plan is in mind. Countless times we have laid down *our* plan in hearing that this is not where the catechumen is (only to pick up the topic again when appropriate). This is threatening to those who have always had the security of the lecture notes from long ago, tried and tested. Flexibility and pastoral sensitivity is essential in the catechumenate.

As time passes the parish rethinks all other forms of catechesis and formation: Confirmation/Reception/Reaffirmation catechesis, prebaptismal catechesis for parents presenting infants, premarital catechesis, Sunday morning Christian Education, how we prepare for death and dying, burial—catechesis in *all* aspects of the parish life. The birth of a baby and the preparation for marriage is often an opening to conversion like the catechumenate. In these cases, life change introduces the ambiguity of joy *and* crisis. Nancy Howell, mother of three children baptized in Grace Church, Galveston, said, "As parents, baptizing our children is a radical act."

In Emmanuel, for part of each session, the catechumenate and the Confirmation/Reception/Reaffirmation catechesis meet together (with clear differentiation of the catechumen and sponsors) beginning with Evening Prayer, followed by an opening reflection on the Sunday liturgy and scripture lectionary for about forty minutes. Then the catechumenate goes to another warm, hospitable room to continue this reflection or to take another approach depending on the catechumen's needs. (We supplement this with social occasions wherein pastoral catechesis occurs.) Confirmation/Reception/Reaffirmation catechesis develops the reflection session into a more "mystagogical" "catechesis. ("Mystagogical" catechesis reflects on the mysteries" in Christ revealed in the lifestyle and ministry of the Church, of the events of Holy Week/Easter.) Once again, the candidates may redirect the topic. The catechist must remain flexible.

We are convinced that the candidates for Confirmation/Reception/Reaffirmation are asking different questions because they *are* sharing in Eucharistic life and are raising comparative questions to their previous tradition. Many are also in need of "conversion therapy"[7] (in the words of Aidan Kavanagh) and we take this seriously. Each must make an appointment with one of the catechists to share their story before the bishop's visitation and some more regularly have one-on-one sessions as needed.

EVANGELIZATION: ALL PARISHES ARE CALLED
TO THIS FIRST STAGE OF THE CATECHUMENATE

Even in those places where unbaptized adults are unlikely, the first stage of the catechumenate, evangelization, is a calling for each parish. Are we really the community open to others and seeking their presence? Commonly catechumens come to community by invitation of a person they already know.

"WHAT DO YOU SEEK?"—"LIFE IN CHRIST"

What does the catechumen seek in our parishes? Jennifer said, "To be part of the church"—to belong. Many say "warmth," or "community." Vicky, when asked why she seeks Baptism said, because it "gives dignity." Our current Director of Religious Education, Katherine Long, has come to believe, however, that we can honestly say only that the Holy Spirit brings a potential catechumen to community.

---

[7] Aidan Kavanagh, OSB, "Introduction," *Made, Not Born,* (Notre Dame, IN: University of Notre Dame Press, 1976), p. 4.

Christian Formation of the Parish Community

Can we be all that they seek? No, of course not. There will be disappointment in our lack of community, in the harsh and sinful politics, as the dead and frozen, apathetic, parish carries on. The catechumen, in this discovery of reality, often becomes a prophetic voice in community for mission and outreach, for authenticity. Vicky raised the question continually as to why our parish does not reach out to the poor, the dispossessed, the needy. Now Vicky; her mother, Martha; and the Finance Committee Chair, Connie Vancea are heading up a task force to open up the ministry of outreach in the life of Emmanuel parish.

"COMMUNION" AUTHORED BY GOD
BECOMES "COMMUNITY"

Privatized, individualized spirituality in denial of corporate community is certain to be overcome in the catechumenate. The spiritual warmth in a "communion" authored by God becomes authentic "community."

Sometimes, in parishes lacking community, the catechumenate remains a sub-community of the parish. One of the tasks before us is how to enable the whole parish to experience this without contriving community. We do believe that when parish leadership is involved as sponsors and catechists, the impact is greater.

One of Christine's sponsors, Phyllis Kerrigan, in a move to Nigeria, has offered us some perspectives on how important community is in this journey (from the perspective of her current objectivity, being temporarily apart from Emmanuel). "It is re-emphasized to me as I sit here in Nigeria that our recognizing the historical fact that Christ lived, died and rose again does not make a Christian. We need him first in His real Presence, accompanied by the life and support of our community to help us on our journey. The catechumenate puts that all together for the parish."

WALTER L. GUETTSCHE

Phyllis also evaluates the Sunday morning Christian Education in a similar perspective. "As a parish we have had Adult Forum following the Sunday Eucharist—the catechumen and sponsors amongst the group. The spontaneous offerings (telling our story) of those not sponsors gave added emphasis to the scripture presenting 'the church's story.' This couldn't help but give a feeling of community which was the experience of the Early Church (warts and all)."

ROLE OF SPONSOR: WHAT IS IT TO BE A GUIDE/COMPANION/SPIRITUAL FRIEND?

Cursory relationships do not occur in pastoral catechesis. In the midst of conversion, the boundaries are broken down. In one session of the catechumenate, the topic became the recent suicide of one of the catechumen's family members. It all came out that one sponsor's son was a suicide victim and for another sponsor, his father.

Sponsors are committed to both the catechumen as a person and to the Church as corporate community. The Church selects sponsors wisely following consultation with the potential catechumen as to whom she/he may especially relate, but the priest and supervisor or catechumenate leadership team must make the final decision, in our opinion.

LIFESTYLE/ETHICS: THE CHRISTIAN COMMUNITY BECOMES A ROLE MODEL

The catechumen is often told that she/he has a ministry to the community just by being. One said that he could never understand this until after his baptism. The presence of the catechumen enables the community to come to terms with the role-modeling of Christian faith and lifestyle—an awesome responsibility. The catechumen watches and asks questions. Are we who we say we are?

Christian Formation of the Parish Community

Christian stewardship is quickly clarified for what it is. A reordering of the priorities of life, discovery of life as gift to be shared, is discernible in the lives of those involved in the catechumenate.

DISCOVERY AND EXPLORATION
OF VOCATION/MINISTRY

Lengthy pastoral catechesis leads inevitably to the awareness that the catechumen is in discovery process for a lifestyle and ministry (and so are we). In some parishes, it has never occurred to many that vocation/calling is a lifelong process of exploration and that the Church is an interdependent community of ministry involving the baptized and ordained. It becomes evident that all are to be prepared for ministry, not just those called to Holy Orders sent to seminary. Holy Orders come to be seen not as exterior (to the ministry of the baptized), but all are rooted in Baptism in the discovery of vocation and ministry.

Sponsors are particularly conscious of this reality. Nancy Howell, who was a sponsor in Galveston, proposes that "spiritual direction" be adopted as a normative part of Christian catechesis to enable the vocational exploration. We recommend the book for reading by sponsors, by James Fowler, *Becoming Adult, Becoming Christian.* [8]

LIVING THE PASCHAL MYSTERY

The Great Vigil of Easter was experienced in both Grace Church, Galveston, and in Emmanuel, Houston, initially as a night liturgy with baptism of infants. It was a decision by the congregation to move to a pre-dawn time for the Vigil

---

[8]James W. Fowler, *Becoming Adult, Becoming Christian* (San Francisco: Harper & Row, 1984).

WALTER L. GUETTSCHE

in both parishes. Early Church readings cemented this decision. Once again, the rector facing yet another potentially unpopular decision, agreed enthusiastically in principle, but wondered if the whole congregation would support it. They did.

The Paschal *Triduum* became a powerful whole in both parish congregations. In Galveston, the dark gothic building housed a congregation dwarfed by its magnitude. Good Friday, Holy Saturday, Easter became an authentic death, burial, and resurrection for a congregation all too aware of the bold realities of life and death through terrible hurricanes and personal tragedies. Triumph and hope rise out of this candid environment. Sponsors, other vitally interested parties, even the policeman assigned to be on guard in that inner-city, crime-ridden neighborhood, helped prepare the font at some unbelievably early hour. The experience of the Vigil was transformed to a much more deeply moving liturgy in its pre-dawn time. The utter darkness of that enormous gothic building had all the power of that Good Friday experience of the mystery of death on the cross. All waited longingly during Holy Saturday as the catechumens and sponsors were on retreat. A *transitus* to Easter in the water of that font made the passage known so well to all of us in the lives of Melody, Billy, and John.

In Emmanuel parish, Houston, the experience was equally powerful in a modern building of largely glass windows looking up to the sky behind the altar. In the narthex, the tomb-like font waited for Vicky. Much sound of splash and sight and experience of water in candlelight did come to match her authentic conversion journey over those many months. Or was it *our* conversion journey over those many months we were vicariously experiencing through Vicky?

In the cavernous darkness of Grace Church, Galveston, or in the wooded suburban open environment of Emmanuel, Houston, this tomb-like font became the center of such a new birth taking place in the candidates and in us, the church leadership. I can still remember peering down into that "primordial" water in the darkness before the arrival of the congregation at one of the Easter Vigil liturgies, considering all that was taking place. Yes, it was the new birth of Melody, Billy and John—of Vicky, Christine, and Jennifer—but, it was also, somehow, my own dying and rising, new birth, reception of Spirit, and inclusion into community and it was *everybody's*—vicariously we all have come to truly own our baptism. Now I drive past the small town in Kansas where my grandfather baptized me in the Methodist Church and consider anew the profundity of that mystery which is Baptism.

The immersion baptism of Vicky, like that of candidates in Galveston, was the causing of the body to be bowed forward into the water (at the waist). Thereby, the candidate makes willful assent as the priest with hand on back of the head directs that action. Sponsors continued their well-established gesture of support with hands on shoulders standing beside the font.

In the waters of the font described in Texas many have been baptized. Originally modelled after the one in All Saints', Baytown, this font was built for the baptism of the first catechumen of the Church of the Epiphany in Houston. The Right Reverend Roger H. Cilley, Suffragan Bishop, presided over that Great Vigil of Easter where The Reverend Joseph DiRaddo was then rector. Such fear and anger preceded that immersion baptism that one parishioner damaged the corner of the font so that it supposedly could not be used. Similar anger was manifested in Galveston following the "loan" of that same font to my care and to that of Grace Church.

Christine and Jennifer were baptized by pouring over

WALTER L. GUETTSCHE

that font as they placed their heads over the water by standing on the ladder. Christine's son, Eric, was baptized at the same Vigil by pouring. Other children have been baptized in this font, in one case, combining immersion and pouring.

The small octagonal font in Emmanuel is used on the other baptismal days and at the later, more formal, Easter liturgies. (One of the reasons why all of this has been so successful has been the decision to give people options, but not to compromise the integrity or the centrality of what we are saying and doing. As well, the related decisions underscore the foundation of Baptism and the corporate community's role in it.)

It was in the course of using the *Ashes to Easter* curriculum of "The Liturgical Conference" that the symbol of water became so important to the congregation. When a crystal bowl of water was placed in the back of the Nave as the symbol of the week on the First Sunday of Lent, some members of the congregation requested that it remain. As Baptism became more prominent and clearly initiatory and life-transforming, then the congregation wanted the font in the center aisle and the bowl of water in it clearly providing a tangible baptismal symbol to touch and see all the time. Many members of the congregation touch the water on "entrance and dismissal—not the magic superstition of holy water," but getting in touch with our life-giving share in the Paschal Mystery of Jesus Christ which is basic to our life as Christians.

What is it really to live the Paschal Mystery? For the rector of a parish, it is giving up the American "success" story preached by the popular culture, and within the Church as well. Quantity in numbers of people and in finances are priorities for many of us if we want to be successful. Vulnerability and authenticity—not power, control, accomplishment in balance sheets and "glossy" programs—is the way of the cross. Power it is, but not the worldly, successful power the Church sometimes demands that the institutional leaders of the Church must be.

Shortly after Vicky's baptism, a man in the parish made an appointment to see me in my office. On arrival, he presented me with a list of grievances against me neatly assembled on a home computer and numbered. Glaring out from the page was the "immersion baptism" and the "font." These were seen by the man as failures in "incentives" for the congregation's success (and mine).

The leadership the man called for was the safe, secure, "corporate" America image brought into the parish in that homogenous neighborhood of that time (no longer the case now with high rise buildings going up around us and economic crisis, jobless executives, etc.). Without Vicky, would I have played it safe longer? Would the parish? We can only speculate, but the call to prophetic ministry was never so apparent.

Countless clergy tell us that they really do not believe in private baptisms and in expeditious adult baptisms with little or no time for catechesis or formation (saving embarrassment of the candidate whose parents slipped somehow in getting them baptized), but they are being "pastoral" in continuing the practice. Living the Paschal Mystery is risky, and one can be "crucified" by an otherwise loving congregation. Can we really grow if we refuse to move out of our comfort zones?

WALTER L. GUETTSCHE

THE GREAT FIFTY DAYS OF EASTER:
MYSTAGOGICAL TIME

The Great Fifty Days of Easter have become a time for exploration of vocation and ministry in parish life. While the "neophyte" and sponsors enter "mystagogical" time, allowing the mysteries in Christ to be revealed, the broader parish community has discovered this purposeful time as well. "Experience/reflection" catechesis allows the power and mystery of the events of Holy Week through the Vigil to unfold. The neophyte and sponsors meet in their customary small groups, enabling continuity with the bonding established. Psychologically this is essential following such a lengthy time frame with the building-up to Baptism. Otherwise, all involved can "crash," feeling bereft and cut off like the day after Christmas or after returning from holiday travel.

The larger parish community in Emmanuel explores the events of Holy Week in a three-part series using the method developed by Sister Jean Campbell, OSH. The three questions, in a small group reporting environment, center images, phrases, experiences through the Vigil: "Who do we say God is? Who do we say we are? What difference does this make in our life?" Obviously, the outcome is different each year as the words of scripture and experience and participation in the process vary. In 1988, the parish plans to develop this one step further with an all parish "Ministry Conference" on a Saturday during Easter for further exploration of vocation and ministry.

SUNDAY LITURGY: TRANSFORMED COMMUNITY

The faces of the baptized coming to Communion prior to the catechumenate and to renewal in liturgy were often pained, penitential, carved in stone. The "icons" of Christ in the radiant faces of Melody, Billy, John, Vicky, Christine,

Christian Formation of the Parish Community

and Jennifer suggested that we share in the same baptism in culmination of so much life change. Privatized, wooden liturgy has become corporate. In Communion now we see relaxed faces, peace in eyes; redemption is believable.

It seems not accidental that Emmanuel parish adopted as a "Statement of Purpose" at their January 30, 1988, Program Council (all officers): "Seeing and Serving Christ in Ourselves and Others by Offering a 'Community' that grows out of 'Communion.'" Many of those who wrote these words were formed and shaped by the catechumenate.

A catechumen watches. Does this community really mean it when the sign of Peace is exchanged? What is the commitment to be a reconciling community of people who know that their only power for healing and redemption comes from the Cross and Resurrection of Jesus Christ?

CHOICE OF COMMUNITY OF FORMATION

Recently it has come to our attention that it is possible to choose a conflicting community of formation without knowing it. Many subcultures exist both within and outside the Church—apparently harmless.

What this suggests is that the injunction so apparent in Hippolytus of certain conflicts in vocation is to be considered by all of us. We are formed and shaped by ritual actions often so subtle, we are only aware when they become a conflict.

HOW CAN A PARISH PLAN TO MAXIMIZE THE POTENTIAL FOR PARISH FORMATION IN CHRISTIAN INITIATION?

Three levels of effect in parish life can be discerned. First is the catechumenate itself—the catechumen, sponsors, and catechists. Following the Admission of Catechumens, the

WALTER L. GUETTSCHE

"public" involvement (other than with the Confirmation/Reception catechesis) is not substantial until Candidacy for Baptism during the Lent preceding Easter Baptism. Our experience tells us to deliberately allow the catechumenate to develop without public pressure (sometimes the catechumen is most vulnerable with personal life stress). Large crowds can inhibit bonding and contrive the process toward a programmed time frame. We tell the catechumen before admission that we will not pre-determine which Easter will be the baptism. It is up for decision by the catechumen (sometimes wanting more time), and is a decision made together with their sponsors and the leadership. In a small mission congregation, the potential for greater involvement on the part of the congregation may be greater (especially in the catechetical dimension).

Secondly, those leaders in formation by the catechumenate (sponsors, catechists) enter into ministry with other people in the parish, often without knowing it. We have found that involvement of the leaders and "business-type heads," if possible, alters the parish perception positively and increases the impact on the parish life.

Finally, the general congregation benefits from a transformed sense of liturgy planning, social life, catechesis, and substantial sense of interdependent ministry. Usually, they are quite unaware of the source of these newfound perspectives until we do a session on the catechumenate in the general parish.

4. Crisis in the Catechumenate

Crisis, conflict, chaos, uncertainty, disagreement, discouragement are a normal part of the life of a healthy catechumenate. When everything is calm, unemotional, contrived, static, we wonder if any conversion or transformation is really in process.

Christian Formation of the Parish Community

On the other hand, some crises are not needed. *Never should agitation to conflict be precipitated by the catechumenate leadership. A warm, loving, consistent catechesis is enough as catalyst to a conversion process.*

As well, crises within parish life of drug and alcohol dependence, mental illness, personality conflict, self-identity uncertainty, marriage and relationship conflict, are inevitably found within the catechumenate.

The leadership team must assess the situation when crises appear to determine what action to take. It is evident, in retrospect, that a professional in drug and alcohol abuse was badly needed in one case. The leadership may also need to consult with mental health professionals or supplement the catechesis with the expectation that one-on-one therapy occur when required.

Sponsors may manifest some of the catechumen's weakest points at times, as well. In general, sponsor training, preparation, and commitment are imperative. *The greatest enemy of the catechumenate is lack of commitment, involvement, understanding, and any formation on the part of sponsors.* It should be said, however, that sponsors may be highly inexperienced in that relationship (though mature Christians), yet grow during the journey together in a profound way.

5. *Parish Inhibitions to Effective Christian Initiation*

We have already explored the inherent crisis of baptism into unformed community or even non-existent community. Confusion about the nature of the Church as community can seriously inhibit the catechumenate. Unformed community is inherently innocuous: indistinguishable from the world, safe from values conflict.

As previously stated, the insistence that no change in private baptism and lack of catechetical preparation is being "pastoral" is a disservice to the community itself and to the calling to serve the Gospel. A parish engaged in the catechumenate, but doing private baptisms on demand, is doomed to failure. Great potential lies in developing the "baptismal days" (of Easter, Pentecost, All Saints' Sunday, The Baptism of Our Lord, and Episcopal Visitation) as major corporate occasions.

Baptized children treated as "catechumens," ostracized from Communion, is the death of viable Christian Initiation. Respect for our unified initiatory rite wherein Baptism, Consignation, first Communion are whole and complete gives a clear message about the connection of Baptism/Eucharist to all.

Adoption of *some* of the Roman Catholic parish models for catechesis of the baptized seeking Reception or Confirmation can be deadly to our perception of the integrity of Baptism and Eucharistic life if these candidates are treated as catechumens. (Especially tragic is the dismissal of the baptized from Communion for catechesis, or failing to distinguish candidates from unbaptized catechumens.)

All issues of values and lifestyle formation will come to be seen as part of the "whole." A parish which refuses to encourage human values, inclusiveness, and interdependent ministry in respect to the appropriate callings of the baptized and ordained can forget about having an effective catechumenate.

Emmanuel, Houston, could not continue the practice of its early days of banishing women to the Altar Guild and to a separate women's organization. As our practice of Christian Initiation developed, women became lay readers, lectors, Lay Eucharistic Ministers, acolytes, ushers, etc. Baptized children were once dismissed before Communion.

Christian Formation of the Parish Community

Values change as pastoral catechesis develops. Racist jokes and remarks disappear and are no longer acceptable at parish social events. Difficult tests have come our way over issues such as AIDS, divorce, singles. At one time several years ago, a divorced woman was told that the Altar Guild would be having a social event with husbands, but since she was divorced, she would obviously not be coming. Such a spirit of judgment can not stand up in this environment, but if deemed acceptable is a threat to valid evangelization and parish formation.

Such transformation in community values cannot be attributed to the catechumenate, *per se*. However, we do believe that the catechumenate became the *opening* through which leadership begins the rethinking, values clarification process. In addition, the congregation becomes more capable of assessing issues facing them. When "power plays" and other customary church "games" are played, the formed community has tools to interpret.

Parish life in a large multiple-staff environment can easily compartmentalize. Christian Education departments often are not involved in the corporate liturgy and its planning at all. Probably the catechumenate was an opening to exploration and development in this area. Now our Director of Religious Education, Katherine Long, participates regularly in the children's sermon at our nine o'clock liturgy with the homilist. Sometimes the Director of Music, Jon Trapp-Cordova, participates as well (in addition to his other catechetical ministry in music with the congregation).

Hostility to the catechumenate will occur, especially when people are confronted with their own need for conversion and authenticity. Anger is not uncommon. The parish leadership must be aware of the real reasons people are angry, and remain pastoral. Most of all, acquiescence is a disservice to those threatened, and to the whole parish

WALTER L. GUETTSCHE

and its sense of integrity.

The danger of turning the catechumenate into yet another "program" is the greatest danger of all. <u>The catechumenate is the Church being the Church, not another program of the Church.</u>

6. *Where Do We Go From Here?*

RESIST THE TEMPTATION TO
DEVELOP PROGRAMMED CURRICULUM

It would be all too easy for the Episcopal Church to prepare "how-to" guides which include a highly structured and programmed curriculum. Let us pray that the publishers do not decide to market the catechumenate while we are attempting to engage the Church in open dialogue about "pastoral catechesis."

SPIRITUAL FORMATION:
DIALOGUE WITH THE RELIGIOUS

The formation of the person is the formation of community. We have much to learn from the contemplative prayer and spiritual formation tradition. Somehow there must be an interfacing of personal spiritual journey with corporate spiritual journey. Both are needed and the Church must find a way to maintain the integrity of each, but open the dialogue. In Seattle, about two weeks ago, the officers of the Association of Diocesan Liturgy and Music Commissions experienced Compline in St. Mark's Cathedral. While the characteristics violate much of what I have said for some time about corporate spirituality, I experienced the power of that opportunity for personal contemplative prayer in a corporate environment.

In particular, parish life can learn from the Religious. In 1980, I led a two day conference on the catechumenate and

Christian Initiation with the friars of the Society of St. Francis at the Bishop's Ranch. It became evident early on in the discussion that the catechumenate and the novitiate, in accompanying spiritual journey and life change, are closely parallel. I encourage this dialogue to continue with those most experienced in formation in community and its dangers, pitfalls, and joys.

PSYCHOLOGY AND SPIRITUALITY

The potential in dialogue with the psychological community is also evident to me. One of our catechumens came to us by way of a Jungian seminar on symbols and dreams taught by the Dean of Christ Church Cathedral, Houston, The Very Reverend J. Pittman McGehee. In recent workshops with my teacher, Muriel James, the development and formation in "self-reparenting" and in the healing which goes on as the person becomes whole, offers much to us. We have more to learn about transformation from several perspectives.

TRAINING OF LAY CATECHISTS

The development of training for lay catechists is a potential diocesan project, though it is possible in the parish. Emmanuel has been fortunate in having two Directors of Religious Education who are highly competent in pastoral catechesis and not prone to "program" and "compartmentalization." In addition, Paula Martin, our Senior Warden for two years, has been involved in the catechumenate from the beginning with innate skills as a catechist and commitment to continuing education.

ROLE OF THE BISHOP

Bishops can, hopefully, be encouraged that the Church *will* accept their recovered role as chief catechist and officer in

Christian Initiation. The catechumenate will succeed only with the support of the bishop, especially in encouraging the clergy to rethink the practices of Christian Initiation. Successive rectors or vicars can unknowingly destroy the groundwork laid by their predecessor in Christian Initiation when there is no knowledge of the catechumenate or when it is regarded as some esoteric liturgical practice.

"HOW CAN THIS YOUNG WOMAN LIVE IN THE REAL WORLD AFTER ALL THIS?!"

We return to the opening question, "How can this young woman live in the real world after all this?!" Is there not an inevitable conflict with "world" in values when authentic formation in parish life occurs? The result does not have to be "Christ against culture" (in the words of H. Richard Niebuhr)[9] but the ability to live in "world" with clarity, and some appropriate tension (calling for justice, etc.), knowing who and whose we are.

Living the Paschal Mystery (the Way of the Cross) is the way of life for Christians. The parish corporate personality must face this reality. Parishes no less than individuals desire to have it easy, play it safe, and be successful. (Let there be no conflict!) Christians are called to leadership to speak and act for justice, for compassion (to suffer *with*), to care and to live in empathy. Our "country club" parishes desire, at times, to return to a happy innocuous social life where there are no struggles for authenticity in faith and lifestyle. We can ask our catechumen to be and to do only that which we are willing to be and to do ourselves. Immersion into Christian faith and lifestyle is never easy, never popular.

---

[9]H. Richard Niebuhr, *Christ and Culture* (New York: Harper & Row, 1951).

The restoration of the catechumenate is not, somehow, the "magic elixir" to be taken by parishes seeking renewal. A valid catechumenate occurs because the parish leadership has prepared and is ready to meet the challenges presented. The call is to "holistic" lifestyle and valid evangelization.

The catechumenate is, after all, only an *opening* to change of perspective and ways of being and doing. A small group within a large parish *may* be able to enact a valid catechumenate, but fireworks are ahead and much disappointment if there is no baptism into a *community* seeking to unify the perceptions implied.

Finally, those who have quietly benefited from the environment of the catechumenate (without awareness of parish history) sometimes speak most profoundly. At the conclusion to a rather lively discussion in the Confirmation/Reception catechesis about two weeks ago, Richard Bouchard, the father of Emily (a young girl baptized last All Saints' Sunday) approached me and said, "I hope that you know that I am very much involved—thinking much—but I say very little." I told him that I was very much aware of his presence and participation. He said, "I have been sitting here thinking on formation, 'Water has no form in and of itself—community gives form—for Baptism'."

WALTER L. GUETTSCHE

VIII.

Post-Baptismal Catechesis

ROBERT BROOKS

The length of this talk is going to require a great deal of restraint because, as you noticed, the other talks have gone for forty-five minutes to an hour and five minutes, and they were just talking about the year or so that leads up to sacramental initiation at Easter. Now I am supposed to talk about what people do for the rest of their lives, so I am going to be trying to conflate seventy or eighty or whatever years into just forty-five minutes.

We have a new word for you which you've heard thrown around a little bit, and I know that Episcopalians find Greek words difficult. That's why they are in the *Episcopal* Church and have the Holy *Eucharist* on Sunday. They don't like those kinds of words, but this is a word that we need to recover. Some of us over the last few years, including those in the Milwaukee Project with Bishop Roger White, have tried to find a different word that describes what it is. We can't really find one, so we'll just call it what it is and that is "Mystagogia." It is an important word to learn, because it is what the rest of life is all about after you are baptized. And the reason that we sometimes don't know what to do with the Great Fifty Days and sometimes get loose in our language, and call it the Post-Easter Season when it is The Easter Season of the Great Fifty Days, is because we really don't know what mystagogia is. I'm not going to be able to tell you what mystagogia is because I think the Church is trying to rediscover that, but I'm going to suggest some directions that are pointed to by the experience of communities that have been at this for eleven or twelve years. I will also, of course, look at the rites themselves for clues as to what the rest of Christian life might look like.

We've had glimpses of that from Dick Norris and Aidan Kavanagh, and it probably sounded very different from what we have imagined from the past. It is going to be very different, and we want to begin to explore that.

The Great Fifty Days is, in fact, the paradigm for the rest of the life of the Christian. What we say about that time, what we do in that time, who we say the neophytes are in that time, is really a kind of microcosm—a very intense, tightly packed fifty day period that prepares Christians for the remainder of their Christian life.

This is not about the catechumenate or the period of election or candidacy for Baptism. This is living now, having been sacramentally initiated at Easter. This is the clue, the benchmark, the sign—everything that we need to be able to move out—of course, having been well equipped by a thorough, intense, deeply transforming catechumenal period.

So, what is our mystagogia during the Great Fifty Days for the neophytes, and for the community? The agenda for the Fifty Days always in the Church has been to unpack the meaning of what happens to the candidates for Baptism in their baptism at the Great Vigil of Easter. That is why the readings of the 1979 *Book of Common Prayer* lectionary now all point back to the font, and when one has preached those year in and year out with neophytes in the community, one realizes—I suddenly discovered and I'll get into this a little more later—that one's preaching becomes more and more like the Fathers of the Early Church, which was heavily, "As you have seen . . . as you have seen . . . as you have seen," over and over and over again, drawing out the meaning.

It is not that the neophytes are some sort of empty vessel which you must fill with something. As Aidan Kavanagh pointed out, we must not confuse mystagogy with evangelization. They have already been evangelized long ago. This is a process of drawing out the implications and the rich, inexhaustible meaning of the great gift that Baptism is in their lives. Those readings help us to unpack that.

The Great Vigil of Easter came into being as the final, intensive prebaptismal catechesis for the elect. Those nine Vigil readings with the Epistle from Romans and the Gospel reading, and that whole rich liturgy, led them through the Pasch of Jesus in the font. It was the very source of their understanding in a kind of intense, close, clear, defined way of what it meant to be Christian and what it meant to live it out. Aidan Kavanagh would say that the source of our ecclesiology is what we say about those catechumens as they enter the font. The whole complexus of the Great Vigil of Easter expresses to us what it means to be Christian, what it means to be Church, what it means to live the new life.

Mystagogia is all that, and it really does take fifty days at least to unpack it because the meaning is so dense and rich. It is as simple as understanding the four basic elements which the rubrics clearly define. The four major pieces of

Post-Baptismal Catechesis

the Vigil being the Liturgy of Light, which begins with the Paschal Fire and continues on with the deacon's Easter proclamation and the Exultet; then the story telling rite; then the baptismal bath, initiation into the story; concluding with the entrance to the Eucharistic meal.

Nathan Mitchell once said that in the Great Vigil of Easter, the Christian community returns to our most basic roots as human beings. When human beings travelled in earliest times they took with them in their journey: fire, water to drink, food, and their story, so they could share that sense of identity with whomever they met. He says that every Easter, the Christian community once again gathers around the fire to hear the story, to initiate people through water into that story, and to share the community's meal. The Vigil is absolutely taking us to the depths of our humanity and giving it radically new meaning.

The Vigil also is about the transformation of the material universe. Think of the incredible variety of material things that are used in that liturgy: light and darkness, fire, water, oil, bread, wine, bodies—a phenomenal richness of images saying that the whole material universe in Christ has been made a new creation, all of it. So the doctrine of the incarnation is affirmed most explicitly and concretely in the celebration of the Great Vigil of Easter. It tells us something then about our basic humanity, and it tells us something, not only about the transformed human race, but also about an entirely transformed universe caused by the resurrection of Christ. All of creation has been made totally new.

The solemn prophecies are there and they tell us, to quote John the Deacon, "who we are and who we are becoming." Bill Countryman yesterday spoke of the scriptures, the key to understanding, and he quoted some passages from the New Testament, pieces that give clues, the Paschal Story. The Early Church also understood the solemn prophecies to be the key to understanding the scriptures. This is a final, intensive, mini-course in salvation history—the whole sweep right through from creation to "new creation and resurrection. The liturgy is saying, If you haven't quite got it right—you elect—here it is all together in one final, quick, cram course in salvation history. These nine readings, start to finish, that's who you are. That's who you are. You are a new creation, you were made in the image of God, you were brought out of chaos, you are brought to new life, you have crossed through the waters of the Sea of Reeds, you are an Exodus people, you are all of those things that the solemn prophecies point to."

This is the question that we ask in every catechumenal session, it is the question throughout mystagogia: What is the Church saying to us about who we are? What is our dignity as the baptized in the new humanity? It is very, very clear, over and over again. It's as if the Church has an inexhaustible supply of symbols colliding upon one another in almost overwhelming paradox, in order to say, "Get it right . . . get it right . . . can't you see? . . . can't you see what you have become?"

Lent says, "Become," Easter says, "You are." Simple as that. So the solemn prophecies tell us who we are, and they are inexhausible sources for the whole of Christian life; there will always be new meaning as our story intersects those stories.

We also explore the renunciations and the affirmations of the Great Vigil of Easter. We are people who have turned away from Satan and all the spiritual forces that rebel against God. We are people who have turned our back on that. You know, the Early Church literally turned the people around and moved them to another place to make the affirmations so that they acted that out. In fact,

Post-Baptismal Catechesis

they had turned their back on all that was destructive, dehumanizing, anti-God, anti-humanity, as God sees us and has called us and has given us our destiny. The affirmations say that we are people, as Aidan says quoting the New Testament, whose "yes" means yes and whose "no" means no. And we have said, "Yes," and we will say, "Yes," the rest of our lives. In every Eucharist which is a shape of proclamation and response, we always say, "Yes, yes, yes, yes, yes," all the way through.

The baptismal covenant talks about the lifestyle of prayer, communion with others in the Christian community and Eucharistic sharing, of repentance and turning again to the Lord, seeking and serving Christ in all people, striving for justice and peace, respecting the dignity of every human being. You see, the solemn prophecies of the Vigil tell us why we can seek and serve Christ. Seeking Christ presumes there is a Christ to be found in all people. The Vigil doesn't say, "Wait for the Christ to jump up out of the other person, grab you, throw you down and pin you and say, 'Here I am.'

The baptismal covenant calls upon us to commit ourselves to seek the Christ in that person, which is an action, and when we have found the Christ, knowing that the Christ is in all people, to serve that person. That's why we can strive for justice and peace and respect the dignity of every human being, because the dignity does not depend on their credit rating, or where they live or their job; it depends upon the fact that God has put within them eternal life. This is an ontological reality that God has already done and we're simply celebrating and praising that.

We are to be Eucharistic people, people of praise and thanksgiving, and that is why we strive for justice and peace. The dignity is there, God-given. We work within this world—an incarnational, transformed creation—to assist God's action that has already happened for all humanity.

The water rite also is a source for understanding who we are. In the prayer of Thanksgiving over the Water, we hear about creation, the spirit moving over water bringing forth a new creation and a new humanity in God. We hear about Exodus, the people who were called out of bondage and slavery to freedom. Here are keys again to the scriptures, of creation/exodus, creation/exodus, over and over again. We hear of Jesus at Jordan and how the Spirit moved upon him, the Father proclaiming him the chosen one. We hear of Jesus' Pasch, his passage, his passover, his exodus from the slavery of death to the freedom of life through the waters of the tomb font. And then the presider says, "Now sanctify this water."

This is not a God who has to be screamed at, cajoled or yelled at. This is a God who acts consistently to create, to bring an exodus, to proclaim sons and daughters at the water of Jordan, to lead from the tomb to resurrected life. We are getting ourselves into God's rhythm in prayer. It is eucharistic; it is proclaiming what God is already doing. It is epiphany, a showing forth, a manifesting through word and action to the world of God's continuing salvific activity. So now this water will bring the new creation also. This water is Exodus, Sea of Reeds. This water is Jordan. This water is the water of the tomb font that Jesus springs out of to resurrected life.

It is a great and powerful mystery and it is about who these people are, who they have become because of this. And therefore it is that we can praise in the doxological conclusion to that prayer, "Once again, you have created, liberated, brought to resurrection, and we thank you for one more act here in our midst."

Post-Baptismal Catechesis

We don't believe because the Bible tells us so—the little song of youth—but because, as Alexander Schmemann said, we have seen the Christ burst forth from the waters of the tomb font in our midst. It is a present reality. As Robert Taft, Byzantine Rite Jesuit liturgist, has said, the Church always says *Hodie,* "today," Christ has risen, not two thousand years ago. "Christ is risen—wasn't that a nice memory, and aren't we happy for him?" No. It is an embodied reality in our midst in which we can say, "Alleluia, Christ has risen," because we see the Christ bursting forth from the tomb in the bodies of the neophytes. Christ is here in our midst. It is an agenda for a lifetime to unpack that meaning for us.

Consignation and chrismation amplify, enrich, and explicate the meaning of that water rite. Cyril of Jerusalem is getting good press at this conference. He said, 'You are all Christ every one of you,' referring to the neophytes, because they had been anointed with oil.

There are ethics that flow out of that because, Cyril goes on to say, and scripture says, "Do not touch my Christ," that is, my anointed one. If we understand who these people are, if they are the Christ, what does that say about assault on people? What does that say about murder?

I can remember my Altar Guild when I first came to All Saints just being a wreck over what to do with little cotton dobs with chrism on it—you know, "How do we handle this?" The Early Church, in contrast, was very concerned about how we handle the people who had chrism on *them,* and those people were handled with great dignity and honor. It changes your whole perception about what we say about war. I mean, the Early Church considered murder to be sacrilege; it was the desecration of a holy object because these people were the Christ, they were chrismated. It was very obvious.

ROBERT BROOKS

By the Middle Ages, mind you, the Canon Law said, "Sacrilege is if you strike a priest or bishop." The old Code of Roman Canon Law said, "No, it's only bishops." After the war in El Salvador had been going on for some time, Pope John Paul II proclaimed that the assassination of Archbishop Romero was sacrilege. Thousands of baptized had been slain, but only *then* had we finally reached sacrilege. The Church really had a little problem explaining why there hadn't been a lot of sacrilege going on before that. You will be pleased to know that the new Code of Roman Canon Law has pulled the circle a little tighter. Now the only person whose assassination is sacrilege is the Pope.

I think there is a real problem with this understanding of Baptism. We need to push those boundaries back out. There are some strong social justice implications in the meaning of a person who has come out of that tomb, womb, font and been Christed. There is an agenda for a lifetime. The person is brought to the table; in fact, we put them to work immediately in their priestly ministry as the baptized, by mandating they come forth and offer the gifts.

And so they come to the Eucharist, the foretaste of the reign of God, a sign of that banquet of the Messiah which will be at no cost and to which all people are invited. The fact is that the Risen One is still alive because he can still gather his disciples together to break bread with them at table. It is a sign of the resurrection. And the Eucharist is the way that Baptism keeps happening throughout one's life. On every Lord's day we gather to celebrate the Eucharist as the third and repeatable part of the sacrament of Baptism.

Have you ever noticed in the prayer book that the title of the baptismal liturgy is Holy Baptism? Just Holy Baptism. It is really kind of a Tertullian title. Tertullian talked about, as a complete rite, what we would think of as Baptism, Confirmation (or Consignation), and Eucharist. He called that Baptism. Well that is what the Prayer Book does. Remember, at the end it talks about the Eucharist and bringing the gifts, and so forth, and it doesn't seem to say we are stopping Baptism here; now we are going to leap into Holy Eucharist. Holy Baptism in the Prayer Book is one rite, a piece of which is repeatable every Sunday, the day of Jesus' resurrection, the day that he gathered his disciples for a meal.

In virtually every post-resurrection account, Jesus gathers his disciples on the Lord's Day. He appears to them on the Lord's Day, they have a variety of cuisine—fish, bread, whatever—but he gathers them together on the Lord's Day, a sign of his continuing risen presence.

So when I hear—as some people have said earlier this week—that when the Vigil is over then we need to have something else to do with them, I don't know why the something else isn't the Eucharist. The early Church thought it was; Sunday by Sunday, Lord's Day by Lord's Day, throughout life continuing the baptismal mystery on the day of the Lord's resurrection. I can tell you from the experience of living in such a community that once a person and the community have been through the catechumenate and they have appropriated all this, that's what the Eucharist begins to feel like. It really has the sense that it is their first Eucharist; everything that they have been—the whole journey—the whole of it is fed into that first receiving of the Eucharist and it just keeps going.

The Great Fifty Days celebrate an entrance into a new time, of which the Vigil itself also gives us an experience. Some people say that the Vigil is too long, we have to shorten it. You see, that's not what a vigil is. It's supposed to be long, it's supposed to be exhausting, it's supposed to wear down our defenses. Notice that the title is The Great

Vigil of Easter. Somebody thought when they put that title together that it shouldn't be the only vigil of the year. Like the Early Church, we might have vigils on a fairly regular basis. In many places, the Church had a vigil of the Lord's Day every week which was known as the Vigil of the Myrrh-bearing Women—a wonderful liturgy—which is in the *Book of Alternative Services* in the Canadian Church: The Resurrection Vigil of the Lord's Day.

The Early Church wanted to keep alive in the life of the community that sense of expectation and waiting and longing, so they had regular celebrations of vigils. The Great Vigil was the biggest one of the year, all night with baptisms at dawn. It said something about time being transformed and about waiting upon the Lord rather than our confecting and programming God—about waiting in hope for God to come among us.

So time itself is changed. Time itself has been transformed and resurrected. Not just the material universe, not just humanity, but time as a sacrament. God acting in time. Haven't you ever noticed how many times the scriptures are at great pains to tell you what was going on? They give dates. They want to let you know that God acts in time, so they create a community that is constantly expectant, looking for God to act here and now because it understands the *Hodie* character of faith. *Today* is the day of salvation, *now* is the time, always expecting. The Vigil creates a community of people on tiptoe of expectation knowing that God will act and that God acts in the midst of the Vigil. The Fifty Days celebrate that new time—fifty days of living as though it is already the reign of God, manifest, proclaimed visible throughout all of creation.

According to *The Book of Occasional Services,* mystagogia is the fourth stage of this initiatory process. "The neophytes concentrate on the meaning of the sacraments and the shar-

Post-Baptismal Catechesis

ing of the fullness of the corporate life of the community." That is a thumbnail sketch of this period, which means you don't talk about the sacraments during the catechumenate. The catechumens haven't experienced them yet. This is the methodology: We affirm experience first, then reflect. Why? Because that's usually what happens in life and we are trying to teach people something to help them contend with things that happen to them. You don't get the chance to walk in to your job knowing you're going to be fired that day and say, "Well let me think about that, let me plan for that now." No, things happen first in life. A year ago I walked outside of my house hoping to go to dinner somewhere, slipped on the ice and broke my arm, and that changed things a little bit.

Seminarians aren't the only ones who should be taught to think reflectively, to make sense, to ask, "How is God acting in things? What meaning can be drawn out of this? How can I face life better? How can I be better equipped to understand how God is acting in life?" The catechumenate is a model of experience first and *then* reflection, so the church does not speak about sacraments until the people have been initiated through Baptism and that concluding part of Baptism which is Eucharist. Mystagogia is about reflecting upon the experience of Baptism and the experience of the Eucharist frequently during those fifty days. In fact, in *Lesser Feasts and Fasts,* there are Eucharistic propers provided for every day of the Fifty Days for your neophytes. Why? Because as John Chrysostom said, it is really one day that last fifty, the Lord's Day of the year—one seventh of the year, as the Lord's Day is one seventh of the week. Easter is the unitive feast; it's one Pasch. So we share our experience of the sacraments. It is a continuing Eucharist and the fullness of life of the community. This is where Episcopalians should do very well, because it means having a big party, sharing the life of the community, and becoming socially integrated into the community in a new way to celebrate that festivity.

In my parish, we had a lot of blessings of homes at Easter to celebrate the presence of the Risen One. The life of the community included going around from home to home and having this through the Fifty Days. After a few years, we found that Sunday attendance did not taper off at all during those fifty days. It was generally larger than during Lent after awhile. The second largest attendance of the year, after the Sunday of the Resurrection Great Vigil, was the Second Sunday of Easter, which some people still call Low Sunday (but the Prayer Book doesn't). It was a big Sunday—bigger than Christmas. It was also in the Early Church. It was the day that the neophytes came back into the community with their white garments for the final time and received and participated in the full Eucharistic liturgy. Things will change in the life of your community with this.

In talking about the sacraments, of course, there are days when you talk about the sacrament of the Church, again using as a resource the great Vigil of Easter. What does it mean to be Church? Walter Guettsche mentioned yesterday Sister Jean Campbell's notion that you can ask the liturgy the question, "Who is God? Who are the baptized? What is the world, and how do they relate to one another?" And those are the questions you keep asking over and over and over again. What is the Church saying in this liturgy, the Vigil. The whole thing is about who God is, who we are, who Jesus is, what the world is and how we are all related. So we need to spend time talking about the sacrament of the Church and Christ as the Sacrament of God.

What is the context of the reflection on the Great Vigil of Easter? The same as the one during the catechumenate. It is again scripture, prayer, worship and continuing social

Post-Baptismal Catechesis

service/social justice. The rubrics of the catechumenal rite, remember, provide that people are assigned to do apostolic work during the catechumenate. They are already involved in servant ministry. They are in a life-style already which their sponsors can testify to, and which they have to according to the rites of the catechumenate on the first Sunday of Lent. They don't start this during the Great Fifty Days—it began before that. They continue and deepen that and also look again more thoroughly at how their vocation, their own occupation, is itself an arena because they know space has been transformed; the material universe and time have been transformed. "How has this oil refinery been transformed? Where can I see God work? How can I see God work? How is my life transformed, my home environment? God must be acting here; where do we find God?"

So the curriculum again for this (and it's so hard not to say, "Let's have everything in lockstep with a beautiful blue binder," but it's again remembering who these people are, and their dignity, and the fact that God is acting in them and we are trying to put ourselves on God's timetable in their lives) is the story of the people of God, that is, the scriptures and our own stories. So if you want to pick up a book, pick up the Bible; that's the text book with our story.

The story is going to be different each time, which is why you don't have to worry about how this goes on through the rest of life, because all life changes. If I preach—even with a three year cycle—and I come back to readings that I preached three years ago, I just can't even imagine how I would have talked about what I was doing, or where the community was then, or what was going on around them in relation to that story. It's different.

Stories that are truly transforming are like that; they are inexhaustible. This is why the couple on their fiftieth wedding anniversary can still tell the story of how they met and

ROBERT BROOKS

it isn't boring, because they've lived all this life—all the disagreements, and the fights, and the joys, and the triumphs, and the hurts, and everything else, and the anxieties—all the way through the fifty years that started with the one story (the primordial story, if you will) that formed the community, in this case, of two people. And so they tell the story and they have "our song" played, which is what the Church does when it has the responsorial psalms and canticles of the Great Vigil of Easter, and they have the meal that they had then. That is what we do at the Eucharist which is drawn from our primordial story. It is inexhaustible, and it just goes on and on and on.

Again, the methodology is experience first and then reflect, because that is what life is, and we want to equip people for life. Therefore they're not helpless before things, and can make sense of them in the context of the story of Jesus dead and rising.

So what are the readings of the Fifty Days that help to unpack the Great Vigil of Easter? We have the first readings, classically and normatively in our lectionary, being the readings from Acts. What makes those stories amazing is that they have the different disciples healing people and they are amazed. "Oh my goodness, we're doing what Jesus did." You got it. He is still alive in the church. His ministry continues embodied in us. We are empowered with his power through the Spirit of the Risen One living in the community. That's why we tell those stories for fifty days, because this isn't just Jesus any more, except it *is* Jesus now doing exactly the same things. The disciples (and now we) say, "Those sound awfully familiar. Didn't Jesus do these things? And now we're doing them too!" So that's why we read Acts, because the Acts of the Apostles are still going on; it's our continuing story, we're part of it, we are the embodiment of it in our time.

Post-Baptismal Catechesis

The Gospel readings unpack the Great Vigil. The story that is read as the Gospel story on the Second Sunday of Easter every year in any cycle is, of course, the story of the Upper Room. I never really understood a piece of that until we had our first catechumen. I think the Early Church, by mandating that Gospel, was expressing a pastoral concern for its neophytes. Midway through Easter week, Gary—our first catechumen—suddenly had this terrible feeling that he had made a big mistake, and he was terrified. He withdrew way back, like that story about a bunch of disciples who had just experienced the resurrection and whose response to it was to go lock themselves in a room and not go out. Let me tell you, that speaks to neophytes like you wouldn't believe. Remember that this is the *Dominica Albi*, the "Sunday in White," when the neophytes come back in—reaching out for that "oh boy" sort of experience that follows this great event of their initiation. But of course it's also about an inspirited humanity that is sent in peace and is sent out into the world to continue Jesus' ministry. With new humanity in Genesis, and now with the second humanity, the now Risen One blows his breath into them and sends them out embodied with the Spirit. This reading tells us something again about who we are as this new humanity that we saw in Baptism.

The Third Sunday of Easter is always a Eucharistic discourse. This is not accidental; it is because, again, the Church understood that we don't talk about it until the people have experienced it. So now we will talk about it. We can say again "as you have seen . . . as you have seen," and open up the meaning of the Eucharist.

The Fourth Sunday of Easter is always part of the Good Shepherd discourse, so we've got something about ministry again here—servant ministry, shepherding one another. For those of you who have had the privilege of experiencing a catechumenal invitation, where the catechumen is not told what is going to happen but is led through it by the sponsors who know very well what is going to happen, you have a tremendous sense of shepherding. Someone new to our parish came in and saw the initiation of our first catechumen—stumbled in on it and did not know anything was going to happen. The one thing that struck her over and over again was the way in which there was this nurture, care, attentiveness, and support from the sponsors. It was shepherding, the liturgy of how we do that with one another within the life of the community. This is part of the mystagogia of the Fifty Days.

Then we move into those next few Sundays where we anticipate Ascension Day, then celebrate it, and we talk about Christ's lordship over all. We go back to the whole transformation of all of creation and all of time, infusing that with the Risen, Ascended, exhalted life of Christ. And so finally we come to the mystery of the Spirit in the Church and the world, as the sign of the new creation and the new humanity, as we come to the Gospels regarding the Spirit on the day of Pentecost. In so dealing with that aspect, we keep referring back to the Great Vigil of Easter and opening that up in the context again of the scriptures, and also prayer and of worship, and of continuing servant ministry within the life of the community.

See—and you thought there was nothing to do during the Fifty Days of Easter! There's plenty to do; there's a whole agenda there, but it is again—as I say—a paradigm, a microcosom of the whole of the Christian life.

So how do we build communities that continually draw out the new meanings of Baptism, the deeper meanings of Baptism? How do we have mystagogia for life? Wayne Schwab, the Evangelism Officer of the National Church, is considering producing a resource in another year on the church school as mystagogia—new understanding of church school.

What we need is a change of perception, then, about the baptized. They are not imbeciles or mentally deficient people who need to be helped along. They are these people who are the new humanity and the new creation; sons and daughters; heirs co-reigning with Christ; royal, priestly, holy, off-spring of the Divine One. Those are the terms we throw around loosely all the time, but if we really think about them, they are pretty substantial. That's who the People of God are. So we need a whole change in our perception about those who comprise our community; we need to look at people differently; and we need to begin to see that it is possible to have mystagogical communities, to have communities where the very life of the community—the very pattern and rhythm of its existence—draws meaning out of one another at any age, draws out new understandings and new insights into the rich meaning of our baptism.

Eucharist is the third and repeatable part of Baptism and so, of course, all the baptized receive communion; we do not excommunicate the baptized because of their age or whatever other excuse might be found. I remember a situation in which a mother had a two year old daughter, who, of course, had been receiving communion for the two years since she had been baptized. On this particular Sunday the child had been very excited about Eucharist, and the mother could bearly contain her as the Eucharistic Prayer was coming to its conclusion. Then the little girl just ran up to Communion and put out her hands, laughing with joy and expectation. And her mother came up to me in tears and said, "My daughter just taught me something about the Eucharist. I didn't really realize that it was to be received with joy." Now who's educating who there? That's a mystagogical community where even the baptized of very young age are teaching people about the meaning of their baptismal life. So parish life is clearly centered at the font in this restored process in the church. There is not fragmentation of parish life, but everything is brought into relationship.

I would like to reflect on how this would effect a few of the things that we have in the life of our community. How will it change the liturgical year as we discover that the heart of the year is the Triduum. That's the original season. We wouldn't put Advent first; we would put the Paschal Triduum first, so we would see that the whole year is really leading up to and recovering from the Easter Vigil. It is the Church's new year. As Schmemann said, the Church is reborn out of the waters of the font every year at the Great Vigil of Easter—the whole Church. Now that's an awfully interesting theological statement, perhaps even lovely. Can it happen? Well, let me tell you a story of a five year old in my parish in Bay Town, Texas.

This little girl used to talk about things with other people and people would say, "Well didn't you all go on a vacation to California one summer?" And she said, "Yes, we went on the California vacation the year that Gary was baptized." "And then where did you all go next year?" "Well, we went to Hawaii. That was the year that Judy was baptized." Now she hadn't read the Fathers of the Church. But she was dating everything in her life in relationship to a year beginning and ending with initiation of catechumens in the font. That was coming from a five year old. She is not supposed to tell us or educate us about anything, remember. We have to educate her. But she educated us a lot in our understanding of the year beginning and ending in the font: moving toward, recovering from. We will begin to see Lent/Easter as one season. Lent again, as I said, is a season which says, "Become. Become what God has revealed as your destiny and dignity." And Easter says, "You are that," and celebrates it.

Preaching will change. I remember reading an article in a magazine about preaching that said that the preacher felt that he had two good sermons and he just basically reworked them all the time. I found after this initiatory process was restored in our parish that there is really one sermon, which is Jesus' death and rising, experienced in Baptism so that it is concrete and visible. It has a name, and a face, and a story, and a history in the life of the catechumens and the neophytes, and all the Sunday lections really have this as their root—they flow from the Paschal mystery. So we are either preaching to prepare candidates for Baptism throughout the year, or we are drawing out the implications of what has happened in their baptism. That's mystagogia.

Christian education changes. The catechumenate is the model, and it's about formation, not about information. It's about catechesis in a fourfold purview of scripture, prayer, worship, and social justice/social service. That is always the purview, and one must again not confuse evangelism with mystagogia. The baptized have a right to mystagogy to draw out the meaning of who they already are.

There is a presupposition, as Walter Guettsche mentioned, that influences all aspects of education. For example, in premarital counseling, there is an expectation that these people are going through some kind of radical change in their life routine. Two people are now coming together to form one household. They need to reflect on that in terms of the story and in prayer, the worship of the local community, and, as the marriage rite clearly understands that marriage is a ministry to the world as well as to each other and to the church, so there's social service/social justice involved in marriage.

ROBERT BROOKS

The same thing is true with preparation for Confirmation. Our church has now provided some rites that lead candidates toward reaffirmation of the baptismal covenant, by reflecting upon their story, their prayer, their worship, social service and social justice.

Our ministry to the sick changes, helping them to make sense of their illness and to see that their very illness which puts them in hospitals is itself a service to others. That is why we anoint them and make them Christ once again. We remind them that they are the Christ, showing that through suffering there is triumph, and so they minister to others. So all of those aspects are part of that. We learn to be people of God at the time of death, so all of education—if you want to call it that—is mystagogy, drawing out this new story. Illness and death are part of the curriculum of our continuing life story going along as it engages the story of Jesus' death and rising.

Evangelism also is transformed and made concrete, because we are inviting people into a journey in which a whole community is at their service. One of the ways in our society that we can tell people they are important is by spending time with them. When you suddenly see that these people are now at the disposal of God's timetable, for however long that takes—that you are sponsors for the rest of your life—you have made a strongly countercultural statement, and that is a very concrete side of evangelism.

The catechumenate, as you have heard, is a catalysis at the heart of the community. I suggested to the Standing Liturgical Commission when I was a consultant to the rites of the catechumenate in *The Book of Occasional Services,* that they really ought to put a surgeon general's warning on this thing and say, "If you don't want your parish to change, stay away from this, because it will bring about changes in everything and begin to relate things to one another." It renews the community and gives us something to share with others. So the whole concept of ministry begins to change.

Realize that it is the catechism that says Baptism is what admits us to ministry in the church, so this is formation for the largest and most important order/ministry of the church. The catechumenate is centered in lay people forming others for the ministry of the baptized, which is all of us. It also causes an effect on others who discover their gifts and begin to offer them to the community. That was one of the remarkable things that happened over and over again that I hadn't expected at All Saints in Bay Town.

Its people were blue collar, shift workers. Some didn't think they were worth anything, and suddenly we said that Baptism confers gifts. The question is not, "Do you have any?" but, "What are they?" People who said, "I'm just trash," were suddenly getting a very different message. This can cause a crisis in them, as they come to grips with the fact that they actually have gifts. It's a little frightening, because they were always told that they wouldn't amount to anything. God in the baptismal liturgy tells them that now they amount to a very great deal.

This leads to external ministry outside of the local community. Baptism, again, is the way we enter ministry in the Church, and we begin to see our job and the encounters with friends and others as an arena of ministry. Again, because the universe has been transformed, we expect God to be acting, and we know that God will be there in our job situation, in our home environment.

So the question is, "What is God doing?" Well, He's got to be doing creation/liberation kinds of things. Creation/exodus is the kind of key—if you will—that the Great Vigil of Easter gives. So where does it happen? How can we point to it and draw it out? Thus, in our lives, we help others to discover their destiny in the human race.

What about prayers? As we have pointed out over and over again, one of the aspects of the catechumenal formation purview is formation in Christian prayer. The Church is saying that it is not just for a few people, the Prayer Book types. It is saying that it is so basic that your sponsors have to testify before God and the community on the first Sunday of Lent that you've been doing it. So that's sort of an irreducible mark of what it is to be baptized: that you are in the continuing prayer of Jesus and that you embody it somehow. This changes our whole understanding of prayer in the community, and it might lead—as William Countryman mentioned—to the restoration of the Daily Office. It certainly did in our community, because people wanted to have more occasions to pray.

Our common work for social justice also becomes transformed. It will no longer be perceived as only for those people who never outgrew the sixties—the social justice community who we let do their thing—because, again, one of the four elements of the catechumenate is that people are assigned to apostolic works of social justice and social service. On the First Sunday of Lent, sponsors have to be able to testify that the catechumens have been doing that before they can be called to Baptism. The Church is saying that this is basic. You can do marriage encounter, and Cursillo, and stewardship campaigns, and all of this if you want, but these rites are saying that there are four elements that ought to be marks of all the baptized.

There will be people who know the story, and there ought to be people who will offer true worship to God, through the worshiping assembly as Jesus did. They will continue to image forth the prayer of Jesus which was part of his ministry. He was seen praying constantly, or he withdrew to pray, offering prayer to the Father, and so his Body continues to do that. That's how we know that his ministry is still here: he's doing the same thing. Remember the Acts of the Apostles? They went forth on social service/social justice, encountering Christ in the poor, the outcast, the oppressed—not bringing Jesus to them, but discovering Jesus in them.

These are the four marks, if you will, that are there, and they are right there in the rubrics of the rites.

We have approved, as I said, new rites for the baptized who are coming to the reaffirmation of Baptism, to help them as they come from different backgrounds to go through a process. Again, the four elements are there. They encounter scripture, but it's mystagogical. We are not trying to make them Christians, we're helping them to discover a model that could be understood of those people who are coming to us. It might be a kind of Prince and Pauper story. I would hope the community would have this kind of stance. The crown prince comes to the castle dressed in rags of the pauper because he's got a kind of spiritual amnesia—he's forgotten who he is. He comes in and the folks in the royal court recognize the crown prince and say, "Oh my God, you're back. Come here and take all that is your due. Put on those royal robes, put on that crown and get on that throne and let's have the royal banquet." We've made a statement in the teachings of the Prayer Book that Baptism is full initiation. Now, that means that this has already been conferred, not by something that we have done, but that God has acted in that person. That's why I am using "crown prince" here, because that is the language of the New Testament. We just don't think of it that way, you know—co-heirs, already reigning, royal, priestly—all that kind of imagery. We treat them that way, not like "Oh, gee, you have missed out on it, and we're going to flog you to death," but "look at who you are because of the way we receive you and the way we respond to you."

In these rites we use the same catechumenal methodology: experience first and then reflect. This open-ended timetable is as long as it takes for the person. The fourfold shape forms the context: scripture, prayer, worship, social justice. The curriculum is the lectionary and life. There are stages, both for these adults and for parents of children who are going to be baptized, that culminate in rites—stages of formation that culminate in rites.

I think that the best way to conclude is with a quotation from John Chrysostom, to again hold up for us how the Early Church was steeped deeply in a baptismal discipline of the catechumenate, how it was living forth life in mystagogical communities, where in everyone the life and the very rhythm of life in the community was opening up more deeply the understanding of Baptism. John's quotation on the honors of the baptized would be a good reflection for us to carry forth from here, and to help us realize that we are always understanding more deeply who we are.

He said to them, "You are not only free, but also holy. Not only holy, but also just. Not only just, but also sons and daughters. Not only sons and daughters, but also heirs. Not only heirs, but also brothers and sisters of Christ. Not only brothers and sisters of Christ, but also joint heirs. Not only joint heirs, but also members. Not only members, but also the temple. Not only the temple, but also instruments of the spirit. Blessed be God who alone does wonderful things."

Bibliography

(Editor's note: Many of the resources in this Bibliography were written before the General Convention had made it clear that baptized persons are not catechumens. Thus they do not always clearly distinquish between catechumenal processes and the Catechumenate proper. This is particularly the case with many of the Roman Catholic resources since that church treats persons baptized in other traditions as catechumens.)

Associated Parishes, Inc.
> The Great Vigil of Easter: A Commentary. Alexandria VA: 1977.
>
> Celebrating Redemption: The Liturgies of Lent, Holy Week, and the Great Fifty Days. Alexandria VA: 1979.
>
> Christian Initiation: A Theological and Pastoral Commentary. Alexandria VA: 1976.
>
> (All Associated Parishes Publications may be ordered from 3606 Mt. Vernon Avenue, Alexandria VA 22305.)

The Book of Occasional Services: Second Edition.
New York: The Church Hymnal Corporation, 1989.

Brooks, Robert J.
> "Reflections on the Adult Catechumenate and Baptism in the Episcopal Church." OPEN (May 1986), pp. 15–18. (Quarterly of Associated Parishes, 3606 Mt. Vernon Ave. Alexandria VA 22305)

"Diocesan Guidelines for Christian Education and Confirmation." OPEN (June 1984), pp. 6–8.

Countryman, L. William
> The Mystical Way in the Fourth Gospel: Crossing Over into God. Philadelphia: Fortress Press, 1987

Eastman, A. Theodore
> The Baptizing Community: Christian Initiation and the Local Congregation. New York: The Seabury Press, 1982.

Hatchett, Marion J.
> Commentary on the American Prayer Book. New York: The Seabury Press, 1980.

"Homily Service: An Ecumenical Resource for Sharing the Word."
> The Liturgical conference, Inc. (1017 Twelfth Street, NW, Washington DC 10005). Particularly helpful in preparing catechists to lead scripture reflections.

Kavanagh, Aidan
> The Shape of Baptism: The Rite of Christian Initiation. New York: Pueblo Press, 1978.

Kemp, Raymond B.
> A Journey in Faith: An Experience in the Catechumenate. New York: Sadlier Press, 1979.

Leech, Kenneth
> True Prayer: An Invitation to Christian Spirituality. San Francisco: Harper & Row, 1980.

Made, Not Born: New Perspectives on Christian Initiation and the Catechumenate. Papers from the Murphy Center for Liturgical Research. Notre Dame: University of Notre Dame Press, 1976.

Mitchell, Leonel L.
> Praying Shapes Believing: A Theological Commentary on the Book of Common Prayer. San Francisco: Harper & Row, 1985.

Occasional Papers of the Standing Liturgical Commission. New York:
> The Church Hymnal Corporation, 1987. Especially the papers on Christian Initiation and the Liturgy in Easter Season.

Russell, Joseph P. and Vogelsang, John D.
> In Dialogue: An Episcopal Guide for Adult Bible Study. New York: The Episcopal Church Center, 1986.

Stevick, Daniel B.
> Baptismal Moments; Baptismal Meanings.
> New York: The Church Hymnal Corporation, 1987.

Weil, Louis
> Gathered to Pray: Understanding Liturgical Prayer. Parish Life Source Books. Cambridge MA: Cowley Publications, 1986.

Yarnold, Edward J.
> The Awe-Inspiring Rites of Initiation.
> Slough, Great Britain: St. Paul Publications, 1972.

This Bibliography was drawn in part from: Episcopal Church Center (Office for Evangelism Ministries), **The Catechumenal Process: Adult Initiation and Formation for Christian Ministry.** New York: The Church Hymnal Corporation, not yet published.

Bibliography